Grammar WITHDRAWN

Just as physicians must know the meaning of *fibula*, lawyers *tort*, and builders *mortise* to function in their occupations, so do you, as a writer, need an understanding of the basic terms of English grammar and syntax. This section presents the basic concepts of English grammar in their most commonly known terms, those of **traditional grammar**. Some important terms of **structural linguistics** and **transformational-generative grammar** have been added for readers more familiar with those nontraditional grammars.

G-1. The Sentence and Its Parts

A sentence is a grammatically independent unit of expression, made up of two essential parts called **subject** and **predicate**. In writing, a sentence begins with a capital letter and ends with a period, question mark, or exclamation point.

The Two Main Parts of a Sentence

1. THE SUBJECT. The **subject part** of a sentence (the **complete subject**) is the part naming the person or thing that the sentence speaks about. That person or thing itself is called the **simple subject** (or just **subject**):

[complete subject in italics; simple subject in bold print]
The old **road** *along the coast* leads you to the bridge.
A noted **scientist** *from France* will speak here tonight.
Poor old **Dr. Faust** is finally retiring from the college.

2. THE PREDICATE. The **predicate part** of a sentence (the **complete predicate**) is the part that speaks about the subject. It tells what the subject *does* or asserts that the subject *is* something.

a. The simple predicate: The key word (or words) in the predicate—the word stating the actual doing or being—is called the **simple predicate** (or just **predicate**) or **verb**:

[complete predicate in italics; simple predicate in bold]
The old road along the coast **leads** *you to the bridge.*
A noted scientist from France *will* **speak** *here tonight.*
Poor old Dr. Faust *is finally* **retiring** *from the college.*

b. Complements: A **complement** is a word needed to complete the meaning of some verbs: Sandra saw *Orson.* Macdonald was a *Conservative.* See G-3.3, page 3.

A subject, predicate (verb), or complement may be **compound**; that is, it may have two or more parts joined by *and*, *or*, or *but*:

[compound subject and complement in italics; compound verb in bold]
Poems and *stories* **delight** and **edify** *children*, *teenagers*, and *adults.*

Sentences Are Classified in Two Ways:

3. BY PURPOSE.

DECLARATIVE (a statement): You are my friend.
INTERROGATIVE (a question): Are you my friend?
IMPERATIVE (a command or request): Close the door.
EXCLAMATORY (an expression of emotion): How glad I am!

4. BY STRUCTURE, according to the number and kinds of clauses they contain. A sentence may be **simple, compound, complex**, or **compound-complex**. G-8.6, page 8, explains these categories in detail.

Avoid These Common Errors in Writing Sentences:

5. THE SENTENCE FRAGMENT. A **fragment** is a piece of a sentence, such as a phrase or dependent clause, erroneously punctuated as if it were a complete sentence. A fragment is considered one of the most serious mechanical errors in written English. When you discover a fragment in your writing, either (1) attach the fragment to an independent clause or (2) rewrite the fragment to form a sentence by itself. Even a statement with a subject and a predicate can be a fragment if it follows a subordinate conjunction, such as *if, when*, or *because*. In the incorrect examples below, the fragments are in italics.

WRONG: I was happy. *Because finals were over.*
RIGHT: I was happy *because finals were over.* [fragment attached to independent clause]

WRONG: *An idea that appealed to us.*
RIGHT: *The idea appealed to us.* [fragment rewritten as a sentence by itself]

WRONG: *Walking across the campus.* Ada slipped and fell.
RIGHT: *Walking across the campus*, Ada slipped and fell.

6. THE COMMA SPLICE AND THE FUSED SENTENCE. In these errors (also called **run-ons**), the writer puts two unconnected sentences within the boundaries of one sentence. See explanation in P-1.19, page 13.

The Sentence Pattern

7. SUBJECT, VERB, AND COMPLEMENT(S) occur in a standard order, or pattern, in English: S V (C) (C). This means that usually the subject [S] comes first, then the verb [V], then—perhaps—one or two complements [(C)]. This normal order is sometimes altered, as in interrogative and exclamatory sentences (see 3 above), in sentences such as

    V   S   V S V   C
Here are the books and *Never have I seen such chaos*, and in sentences beginning with expletives (see G-9.9, page 9).

G-2. The Parts of Speech: A Survey

Every word performs one of five functions: *naming, expressing doing* or *being, modifying, connecting*, or *expressing emotion*. In traditional grammar, these functions are classified into eight **parts of speech**: *noun, pronoun, verb, adjective, adverb, preposition, conjunction*, and *interjection*. Learning to recognize the parts of speech will help you write with greater ease, confidence, and accuracy.

1. WORDS THAT NAME.

a. Nouns: A noun is a word that names a person, place, thing, or idea:

PERSON: Maria, woman, Mick Jagger, boy
PLACE: Toronto, Banff, waterfront, earth

THING: shoe, car, dog, carrot, CN Tower
IDEA: love, strength, courage, democracy, height

See G-3, page 3, for details about nouns.

b. Pronouns (*pro-* means "for" or "instead of"): As its name suggests, a pronoun takes the place of (stands for) a noun. The noun that a pronoun stands for is called the **antecedent** of that pronoun:

[pronouns in bold; antecedents in italics]

Sally took three suitcases with **her** to Paris.
When the *Martians* come, **they** may not harm Earth at all.

See G-6, page 5, for details about pronouns.

2. WORDS THAT EXPRESS DOING OR BEING: VERBS. A verb asserts something about the subject of a sentence. It tells what the subject *does* (an **action verb**) or tells that the subject *is* something (a **linking verb**):

ACTION: The arrow *pierced* the target. [tells what the subject, *arrow*, did]
LINKING: The arrow *is* an accurate weapon. [tells that the subject is something]

Some verbs consist of several words: **main verb** + one or more **auxiliary** (helping) **verbs**:

[main verbs in bold; auxiliary verbs in italics]

Aloysius *had* **sought** Fayella in vain.
She *might have been* **thrown** into the river.

The verb in a sentence is also called the **(simple) predicate**. See G-4, page 3, for details about verbs.

3. WORDS THAT MODIFY. *To modify* means "to change." A word that modifies changes or clarifies our concept of another word.

a. Adjectives: An adjective modifies a noun (or occasionally a pronoun). It describes that noun or limits its meaning. **Descriptive adjectives** tell *what kind: small* car (what kind of car?), *green* rug, *unimaginable* brutality, *odoriferous ten-cent* cigar. **Limiting adjectives (determiners)** tell *which one* or *how many*. There are several kinds of limiting adjectives:

POSSESSIVE: *my* auto, *her* grades, *their* policy [which auto, grades, policy?]
DEMONSTRATIVE: *this* auto, *those* grades, *that* policy
INDEFINITE: *any* auto, *either* grade, *many* policies
INTERROGATIVE: *which* auto? *whose* grades? *what* policy?
NUMERICAL: *one* auto, *two* grades, *third* policy
ARTICLES: *an* auto, *the* grades, *a* policy

As in these examples, an adjective usually appears directly before the noun it modifies. A descriptive adjective can appear also after a linking verb (as a complement). Such an adjective describes the subject that it is linked to by the verb:

S   V   C
My car is *small*. [*Small* describes the subject, *car*.]
Our bedroom rug looks *green*.

b. Adverbs: An adverb usually modifies a verb. It describes *how, when, where,* or *to what degree* the action of a verb is done. There are several kinds of adverbs:

MANNER; Brenda drives *carefully*. [drives how?]
TIME: Brenda drove *yesterday*. [drove when?]
PLACE: Brenda drove *everywhere*. [drove where?]
DEGREE: Brenda studies *enough*. [studies to what degree?]

An adverb phrase or clause can also describe *why*.
Some adverbs can modify an adjective or another adverb. Such adverbs are called **adverbs of degree** (or **intensifiers**).

Brenda drives *quite* carefully. [carefully to what degree? how carefully?] She prefers *very* cautious behavior.

For **conjunctive adverbs**, see P-5.2, page 15.

4. WORDS THAT CONNECT.

a. Conjunctions: A conjunction joins other words or word groups. There are two kinds of conjunctions:
(1) A **coordinate conjunction** (*and, but, or, nor, for, yet*) joins words or word groups of the same kind and same importance:

WORDS: Jack *and* Jill
WORD GROUPS (phrases): up the hill *and* into the woods
WORD GROUPS (clauses): Jack fell down, *and* Jill came tumbling after.

NOTE: And, but, or, or *nor* may be used with other words to form a **correlative conjunction**: *not only . . . but also; (n)either . . . (n)or; both . . . and:*

Both Jack *and* Jill went up the hill.
Neither Jack *nor* Jill enjoyed the outing.

(2) A **subordinate conjunction** (*if, because, although, when, unless*) joins a dependent (subordinate) clause to an independent (main) clause. The subordinate conjunction begins the dependent clause: *if you love me; because he wasn't careful.*

If you love me, you will never release that letter.
You will never release that letter *if you love me*.

Do not write a subordinate clause alone as if it were a sentence. The result is a serious error called a fragment:

WRONG: You will never release that letter. If you love me.

G-1.5, page 1, discusses fragments in detail.
Other common subordinate conjunctions are *whenever, while, as, since, before, after, until, as soon as, so that, in order that,* [even] though, whereas, whether, where, wherever, as if, as though, than, provided.*

NOTE: Other kinds of words that join clauses are **relative pronouns** (such as *who* or *which*—see G-8.3, page 7) and **conjunctive adverbs** (such as *therefore* or *however*—see P-5.2, page 15.)

Some authorities call coordinate conjunctions **coordinators** and subordinate conjunctions **subordinators**.

b. Prepositions: A preposition is a joining word such as *in, on, of, for,* or *into* that shows how a noun is related to the sentence that contains it:

The bird flew *into* the cage.
The bird flew *over* the cage.
The bird flew *around* the cage.

Each preposition above shows a different relation between the noun *cage* and the action of the sentence. Other common prepositions are *to, toward, from, above, under, beneath, underneath, below, past, by, onto, upon, behind, beside, through, out* [of], off, between, among, near, next to, in front of, against, about, within, inside, outside, at, up, down, before, during, until, since, besides, except, like, despite, instead of, because of, in addition to, as well as.*

The word group beginning with the preposition and ending with the noun is called a **prepositional phrase**. The noun (or pronoun) is called the **object of the preposition**:

[prepositions in bold; objects of prepositions in italics]

with all her *friends*   **of** the *night*   **for** *me*

5. WORDS THAT EXPRESS EMOTION: INTERJECTIONS. Unlike the other kinds of words, the interjection has little or no grammatical connection with the rest of a sentence:

MILD INTERJECTION (punctuated with comma): *Well*, I wouldn't worry about that.
STRONG INTERJECTION (punctuated with exclamation point): *No!* I can't believe it!

6. SOME WORDS CAN BE USED AS TWO OR MORE PARTS OF SPEECH. The way a word is used in a particular sentence determines its part of speech in that sentence. To determine the part of speech of a word in a particular appearance in a sentence, examine its grammatical use (**syntax**) in that sentence: if it names something, it is a noun; if it describes a noun, it is an adjective; and so forth:

NOUN: Turn on the *light*.
ADJECTIVE: I prefer *light* colors in my room.
VERB: Why didn't you *light* a fire?

NOTE: You can often determine a word's part of speech by its position or its ending. For example, a word following *a, my, this,* or another limiting adjective is most likely a noun (although another adjective may intervene): *My* older [noun] was married yesterday. A word following an auxiliary is most likely a verb: The bill *should have been* [verb] in the House of Commons. Most words with an *-ly* ending are adverbs: *slowly, disgustedly*; words ending in *-tion, -ity, -ness,* or *-ment* are usually nouns; words ending in *-ify* or *-ize* are most likely verbs; words ending in *-al, -ous,* or *-ful* are most likely adjectives.

G-3. Using Nouns

Recall that nouns name persons, places, things, or ideas.

1. KINDS OF NOUNS. Nouns are classified in several ways:

a. Singular or plural: A **singular** noun names one person, thing, etc.: *house, chair, woman, city*. A **plural** noun names two or more persons, things, etc.: *houses, chairs, women, cities*. Most singular nouns become plural by the addition of *-s*. See S-1.6e, page 24, for rules on the formation of plurals.

b. Common or proper: A **common** noun names one or more members of a class of things: *woman, women, chair, auditorium, mice, city*. A **proper** noun names a specific person, place, or thing: *Joan Shea, Carnegie Hall, Mickey Mouse, Vancouver Island*.

c. Concrete or abstract: A **concrete** noun names an object that can be perceived by the senses: *woman, Joan Shea, mice, cheese*. An **abstract** noun names a quality or idea: *liberty, sadness, ambition, love, tragedy*.

d. Collective: A **collective** noun names a group of things: *jury, team, flock, committee, army*.

Nouns Have Five Important Uses.

Recall the basic sentence pattern: S V (C) (C). That is, each sentence has a subject, a verb, and possibly one or two complements. The subject and the complements are usually nouns.

2. SUBJECT OF A SENTENCE. Pattern: S V (C) (C). The **subject** tells *who* or *what* if placed before the verb:

Fred smokes. [Who smokes?]
The *trains* were late. [What were late?]
Sarah and *Ivan* are planning a European vacation. [Who were planning? (compound subject)]

3. COMPLEMENT. A **complement** is a word in the complete predicate that completes the meaning of the verb. There are four kinds of complements:

a. A direct object is a noun (or pronoun) that tells *whom* or *what* after an action verb. Usual pattern: S V C.

I opened the *package*. [opened what?]
The city is employing *teenagers*. [employing whom?]

b. An indirect object is a noun (or pronoun) that appears after certain action verbs, telling *to* or *for whom*, or *to* or *for what*, the action of the verb is done. Pattern: S V C(ind. obj.) C(dir. obj.).

Flo sent *Tony* a present. [sent to whom?]
Tony had done *Flo* a favor. [done for whom?]

c. A subjective complement (predicate nominative) is a noun (or pronoun) that follows a linking verb and renames or explains the subject. Pattern: S V(link.) C.

Henfield was the Liberal *candidate*. [*Candidate* gives another name or title for *Henfield*.]
A kumquat is a *fruit*. [*Fruit* explains what *kumquat* is.]

NOTE: An adjective can also be a subjective complement: Henfield is *unbeatable*.

For a full list of linking verbs, see G-4.2c, this page.

d. An objective complement is a noun that follows a direct object and renames or explains it. Pattern: S V C(dir. obj.) C(obj. comp.).

They called Henfield a *hero*. [*Hero* gives another name or title for *Henfield*.]
The electors declared Henfield the *winner*.

The objective complement occurs most commonly with such verbs as *call, name, elect, designate, consider, appoint, think*.

NOTE: An adjective can also be an objective complement: They called Henfield *heroic*.

4. AN OBJECT OF A PREPOSITION is a noun (or pronoun) that ends a prepositional phrase and answers the question *whom* or *what* after the preposition:

Jeanne lives near *Frieda*. [near whom?]
Smyth did her duty with supreme *courage*. [with what?]

5. AN APPOSITIVE is a noun that follows and renames or further identifies another noun:

Henfield, the incumbent *member*, has been reelected.
That man insulted Prince Karl, the queen's *nephew*.

6. DIRECT ADDRESS. A noun (or pronoun) in **direct address** names the person being spoken to:

NOUN: *Marie*, you've won the lottery!
PRONOUN: Get over here, *you!*

G-4. Using Verbs

A verb is the core of every sentence. Without a verb, a group of words is only a fragment of a sentence instead of a complete sentence. Even if a sentence contains only one word, that word must be a verb: *Run! Wait.* (Every verb must have a subject, expressed or understood. In sentences such as *Run!* and *Wait*, the subject is understood to be *you*.) The function of a verb is to assert something about its subject—that is, to tell what the subject *does* or that the subject *is* something:

Birds *sing*.
The flowers *were blooming* everywhere.
Marie *is* this year's valedictorian.

1. IDENTIFYING THE VERB. There is a simple way to identify the verb in a sentence. The verb is the word that will usually change its form if you change the time of the sentence:

Nowadays I *work* in Don Mills. Long ago I *worked* in Don Mills. Someday I *will work* in Don Mills. For years I *have worked* in Don Mills.

2. KINDS OF VERBS. A verb is classified according to the kind of complement (if any) that follows it. In addition, there is a special kind of verb called an **auxiliary** (or helping) verb that is used together with a main verb.

a. A transitive verb is one that needs a direct object to complete its meaning. That is, it expresses an action that passes across (transits) from a doer—the subject—to a receiver—the direct object:

The batter *hit* the ball. [*Batter* does the action, hitting; *ball* (direct object) receives the action.]
The judge *explained* the rules. [*Judge* does the action; *rules* receives the action.]

b. An intransitive verb is one that does not need a direct object to complete its meaning. It expresses an action that does not have a receiver:

Sally *sneezed*.
Macdonald *died* in 1891. [*In 1891* = prepositional phrase, not direct object.]
Kravitz *obeyed* promptly. [*Promptly* = adverb, not direct object.]

NOTE: Many verbs can be transitive in some uses and intransitive in others. Dictionaries label each meaning of a verb as *v.t. (verb, transitive)* or *v.i. (verb, intransitive)*.

c. A linking (state-of-being, copulative) verb expresses no action at all. It merely expresses state of being; it indicates a link of identity or description between the subject and the subjective complement following the verb:

Foster *is* the vice-president. [*Foster = vice-president.*]
This train *has been* late all week. [*Late* describes *train*.]
Jack *became* a grouch. [*Jack = grouch.*]

The chief linking verb is *be*. Its parts include *am, is, are, was, were, being, been*. Other linking verbs are *become* and *seem* and any that mean roughly the same as *be, become*, or *seem*: *appear, grow, turn, remain, prove*, and the verbs of the five senses—*look, sound, feel, smell, taste*. Some verbs may be linking verbs in one sense and action verbs in another:

Linking	Action
I *looked* disheveled.	I *looked* out the window.
Nancy *grew* pensive.	Nancy *grew* cabbages.

d. Auxiliary (helping) verbs. A verb may contain more than one word, as in *could have helped*. The last word in the verb is the **main verb**. The others are called auxiliary verbs, or simply **auxiliaries**. They convey some condition of the main verb, such as tense or mood. The most common verbs used as auxiliaries are *have, be, will (shall)*, and *do*:

The plane *had left* Alberta.
The plane *is flying* here nonstop.
The plane *will be landing* soon.
The plane *did arrive* on time.
The plane *should arrive* on time.
The plane *must* certainly *have landed* by now. [Note that other words may come between parts of the verb.]
Would either of you not *have offered* assistance?

NOTE: Some authorities call a verb of more than one word a **verb phrase**. Other auxiliaries (sometimes called **modals**) include *would, should, can, could, may, might, must, ought (to)*.

Use Verbs Effectively and Correctly.

3. KNOW THE THREE PRINCIPAL PARTS OF THE VERB. These are the parts you need to know to form all six tenses. They are

	Regular Verb	Irregular Verb
PRESENT TENSE:	play	see
PAST TENSE:	play**ed**	saw
PAST PARTICIPLE:	play**ed**	seen

Regular verbs form their past and past participle by adding *-ed* to the present (with some minor spelling changes, as in *stopped, cried*). Irregular verbs form these parts in various ways. Some change vowels within the verb: *swim, swam, swum*. Some change a consonant: *build, built, built*. Some do not change: *cost, cost, cost*. Some change and add an ending: *break, broke, broken*. Consult your dictionary when in doubt about verb forms, for you cannot safely take one irregular verb as a model for another; consider *make* and *take*.

Some texts and dictionaries give a fourth principal part, the **present participle** (formed with *-ing* added to the present form: *seeing, playing*). It is always regular, except for some minor spelling changes (as in *stopping, loving*).

4. USE THE CORRECT TENSE OF A VERB. Verbs change in form to show the time of the action or linking they express. The six tenses are

a. Present tense (which expresses action or linking occurring now, or ideas that are always true): I *see* him. She *sees* me. Walter *takes* the 8:02 daily. Water *freezes* at 0° Celsius. (Alternate present forms: **Progressive**: I *am seeing* him; **emphatic**: I *do see* him.)

b. Past tense: I *saw* him. She *saw* me. (Progressive: I *was seeing* him; emphatic: I *did see* him.)

c. Future tense: She *will see* me tomorrow. (Progressive: She *will be seeing* me.)

NOTE: In the future and future perfect tenses, many careful writers still prefer to use *shall* instead of *will* after *I* and *we*: I *shall return*. We *shall have left* by then.

d. Present perfect tense (which expresses action or linking in which the past is connected to the present [*perfect* here means "completed"]): She *has lived* here forty years. [She is still living here.] I *have seen* her twice this week. [implying that the action of seeing her (or its effects) is continuing into the present] (Progressive: She *has been living* here forty years. I *have been seeing* her all week.)

e. Past perfect tense (which expresses the earlier of two completed actions or linkings): I said [yesterday] that I *had seen* her [last week]. (Progressive: I *had been seeing* her.)

f. Future perfect tense (which expresses action or linking to be completed before a given future time): She *will have seen* him by Sunday. (Progressive: She *will have been seeing* him.)

5. USE A VERB THAT AGREES IN PERSON AND NUMBER WITH ITS SUBJECT. G-9, page 8, deals with the very important topic of agreement. See also G-6.1, page 5, for an explanation of person.

6. DISTINGUISH A VERBAL FROM A VERB. A **verbal** is a form derived from a verb. It is used not as a verb but as a

noun, adjective, or adverb. There are three kinds of verbals: **infinitives, participles**, and **gerunds**.

a. Infinitive (*to* + verb), used as
(1) noun: *To worry* is futile. [subject]
Toni wants *to travel*. [direct object]
Toni's ambition is *to travel*. [subjective complement]
(2) adjective: This is the road *to take*. [modifies *road*]
(3) adverb: This book is easy *to read*. [modifies *easy*]
She came *to help*. [modifies *came*]

b. Participle, used as adjective:
(1) Present participle (verb + *-ing*):

The *burning* house began to collapse. [modifies *house*]
Burning furiously, the house began to collapse. [modifies *house*]

(2) Past participle (third principal part of verb: for regular verbs, verb + *-ed*; for irregular verbs, no set form but often ends in *-en*):

The *burned* child was given first aid. [modifies *child*]
Badly *burned*, the child was given first aid. [modifies *child*]

c. Gerund (verb + *-ing* ending), used as noun:

Seeing is *believing*. [subject, subjective complement]
They condone *surviving* by *stealing*. [direct object, object of preposition]

NOTE: An *-ing* verbal may be either a gerund or a participle, depending on its use in a particular sentence:

Swimming is excellent exercise. [gerund: used as noun—subject]
The *swimming* child reached the raft. [participle: used as adjective, modifying *child*]

---

7. DO NOT SHIFT TENSE WITHOUT REASON.
WRONG: In chapter 12, Duddy *moved* to the Laurentians and *rents* a house.
RIGHT: In chapter 12, Duddy *moved* to the Laurentians and *rented* a house.
RIGHT: In chapter 12, Duddy *moves* to the Laurentians and *rents* a house.

8. DO NOT OVERUSE THE PASSIVE VOICE. Transitive verbs have two voices. In the **active voice**, the more common one, the subject is the doer of the verb's action: A million citizens rousingly *cheered* the queen. In the **passive voice**, the receiver of the action becomes the subject, and the doer (if mentioned at all) appears in a *by*-phrase: The queen *was cheered* rousingly by a million citizens.

The passive voice is formed from the past participle of the verb, preceded by the appropriate form of *be*: *am cheered, was taken, might have been told, will be shot*. In general, the active voice, which stresses the doer of an action, is more forceful than the passive, which stresses the receiver:

STRONGER: With great difficulty we *reached* the summit.
WEAKER: With great difficulty the summit *was reached* by us.

But when the doer of the action is unknown or unimportant, the passive is the appropriate form to use:

My apartment *was broken* into last night.
Dinner *is served*.
The mistake *was* not *noticed* for centuries.

9. DO NOT SHIFT MOOD WITHOUT REASON. The mood of a verb indicates how the idea of a sentence is to be regarded. Sentences that state facts or ask questions are in the **indicative mood**:

There *are* five horses in the corral.
How many horses *are* there in the corral?

Requests and commands are in the **imperative mood**:

Count the horses in the corral. [*You* is understood as the subject.]

The **subjunctive mood** expresses doubt, uncertainty, wish, or supposition or signals a condition contrary to fact. In the subjunctive mood, *am, is* and *are* become *be*; *was* becomes *were*; *has* becomes *have*; and *-s* endings are dropped from other verbs:

WISH: God *be* with you. Long *live* the queen.

DOUBT OR UNCERTAINTY: If he *were* able to do it, it would take a long time.

CONDITION CONTRARY TO FACT: If I *were* he, I would go.

Use the subjunctive also in a *that* clause when the main clause contains a verb of command, recommendation, or parliamentary motion:

I request that the defendant *have* a psychiatric examination. I move that the meeting *be* adjourned.

10. DO NOT CONFUSE VERBS SIMILAR IN MEANING OR SPELLING. Sometimes substituting a synonym for the verb that is puzzling you (such as *rest* for *lie* and *put* for *lay*) helps solve your puzzle. The following sets of troublesome verbs are explained in U, page 27: *accept/except, adapt/adopt, affect/effect, allude/refer, born/borne, bring/take, can/may, cite/site/sight, compliment/complement, discover/invent, emigrate/immigrate, hanged/hung, imply/infer, lead/led, learn/teach, leave/let, lie/lay, lose/loose, raise/rise, range/vary, sit/set.* The following sets are explained in S-2, page 25: *brake/break, precede/proceed.*

G-5. Using Adjectives and Adverbs

Recall that an adjective modifies (describes or limits) a noun or occasionally a pronoun, and that an adverb modifies a verb or sometimes another modifier (adjective or adverb):

ADJECTIVES: a *red* barn, a *swift* ride, a *happy* woman [descriptive]; *this* isle, *seven* crowns, *some* cookies [limiting]

ADVERBS: The horse ran *swiftly*. [modifying a verb, *ran*]
The horse was *very* swift. [modifying an adjective, *swift*]
The horse ran *very* swiftly. [modifying an adverb, *swiftly*]

Many adverbs are formed by the addition of *-ly* to adjectives: *smooth/smoothly, unforgettable/unforgettably.* An *-ly* ending thus usually signals an adverb—but not always, for *friendly, womanly,* and *saintly* are adjectives. A few common adverbs have the same form as their corresponding adjectives: *late, early, fast.* Some adverbs have two forms: *slow(ly), quick(ly).* The sure way to tell an adjective from an adverb is to determine the word that it modifies: You drive too *fast* [drive how? *fast:* adverb]. You are in the *fast* lane [which lane? *fast:* adjective].

The word *not* is an adverb.

Use Adjectives and Adverbs Correctly.

1. USE AN ADVERB, NOT AN ADJECTIVE,

a. To modify an action verb:

WRONG: He *sure* works hard.
RIGHT: He *surely* works hard.

WRONG: He drives *crazy*.
RIGHT: He drives *crazily*.

b. To modify an adjective:

WRONG: This is a *real* fast car.
RIGHT: This is a *really* fast car.

c. To modify another adverb:

WRONG: She tries *awful* hard.
RIGHT: She tries *extremely* hard.

2. USE AN ADJECTIVE (AS SUBJECTIVE COMPLEMENT) AFTER A LINKING VERB.

Janet is *jubilant*. [*Jubilant* describes *Janet*.]
She looks *happy*. [*Happy* describes *she*.]
The flowers smell *fragrant*. [*Fragrant* describes *flowers*.]

See G-4.2c, page 3, for an explanation and full list of linking verbs. Caution: Distinguish between a linking verb and the same verb used as an action verb.

3. USE *good* AND *well*, *bad* AND *badly* CORRECTLY.

ADJECTIVES (used after linking verb) *good, bad*: This is *good*. I feel *good*. This fish tastes *bad*.

ADVERBS (used to modify action verb) *well, badly*: She sings *well*. I have failed *badly*.

NOTE: *Well* can be an adjective in the limited sense of "in good health": I am feeling *well*. She is not a *well* woman. *I feel good*, on the other hand, refers to any kind of good feeling.

4. USE COMPARATIVE AND SUPERLATIVE FORMS CORRECTLY.

a. Most adjectives and adverbs have three degrees. Note how the *-er* and *-est* endings change the degree:

POSITIVE (modifying one thing or action): hard [My bed is *hard*.]
COMPARATIVE (comparing two): hard**er** [Your bed is *harder*.]
SUPERLATIVE (comparing three or more): hard**est** [His bed is *hardest*.]

Most long adjectives and most adverbs use *more* and *most* (or *less* and *least*) instead of *-er* and *-est*:

beautiful, more beautiful, most beautiful
easily, less easily, least easily

Some adjectives and adverbs use either form:

costly, costlier, costliest *or* costly, more costly, most costly

b. A few adjectives and adverbs have irregular forms of comparison:

good/well, better, best   many/much, more, most
bad/badly, worse, worst   little, less, least

c. Use the comparative (not the superlative) when comparing two things:

WRONG: Of the two, Sibyl is the *smartest*.
RIGHT: Of the two, Sibyl is the *smarter*.

d. Do not use both forms of the comparative (*-er* and *more*) or of the superlative (*-est* and *most*) together. One form is enough.

WRONG: This car is *more faster* than that one.
RIGHT: This car is *faster* than that one.

e. Do not compare adjectives or adverbs that cannot logically be compared, such as *unique, perfect, dead, empty*. A glass is either empty or not empty; it cannot be more or less empty (though it can be *nearly* empty).

WRONG: Our design was *more unique* than theirs. [*Unique* means "the only one of its kind"; things cannot be more or less unique.]
RIGHT: Our design was *more nearly unique* than theirs.

G-6. Using Pronouns

A pronoun substitutes for a noun, so that instead of saying *Homer shaved Homer with Homer's new razor*, we can say *Homer shaved* **himself** *with* **his** *new razor*. The noun that the pronoun substitutes for (stands for) is called its **antecedent**. *Homer* is the antecedent of *himself* and *his*. (Not all kinds of pronouns have expressed antecedents.)

Pronouns share almost all the uses of nouns. (For those uses, see G-3.2–6, page 3.)

There Are Five Main Kinds of Pronouns:

1. THE PERSONAL PRONOUNS. These designate one or more particular persons or things:

Person	Singular	Plural
FIRST [person(s) speaking]	I, my, mine, me	we, our, ours, us
SECOND [person(s) spoken to]	you, your, yours	you, your, yours
THIRD [any other person(s) or thing(s)]	he, his, him she, her, hers it, its	they, their, theirs, them

2. THE INTERROGATIVE AND RELATIVE PRONOUNS.

a. The interrogative pronouns are *who* (*whose, whom*), *which, what.* They ask questions:

Who said that? *Whose* car is that? *What* is the time? *Which* of the cars is his? With *whom* did you speak?

b. The relative pronouns are the same as the interrogative, plus *that* and the *-ever* forms: *whoever* (*whosever, whomever*), *whichever, whatever.* Relative pronouns introduce certain kinds of dependent clauses (sometimes called **relative clauses**):

The man *who called* was angry.
Montreal, *which I often visit,* is an exciting city.
I approve *whatever she decides.*

Use *who* for persons, *which* for things, and *that* for either:

PERSON: The officer *who* made the arrest was commended.
The officer *that* made the arrest was commended.
THING: Newfoundland, *which* I love, is always foggy.
The province *that* I love is always foggy.

NOTE: When *of which* sounds awkward, you may use *whose* with things:

We entered the harbor, *whose* pattern of sails and buoys delighted the eye.

3. THE DEMONSTRATIVE PRONOUNS are *this* (plural: *these*) and *that* (plural: *those*). They point out:

This is my house. The ones I want are *these.*
That is Helen's house. What kind of trees are *those*?

4. THE INDEFINITE PRONOUNS refer to no particular person: *one, someone, anyone, everyone, no one, somebody, anybody, everybody, nobody, either, neither, all, any, both, some, few, many, most, another, others, something,* etc.:

Many will complain, but *few* will act; *most* will do *nothing.*
Someone must do *something,* but *no one* wants to do *anything.*

NOTE: Closely related to the indefinite pronouns are the two reciprocal pronouns, *each other* and *one another.* See U, page 29.

5. THE REFLEXIVE AND INTENSIVE PRONOUNS are the *-self* forms of personal pronouns: *myself, yourself, yourselves, himself, herself, itself, ourselves, themselves.*

a. They are called reflexive when used as objects or as subjective complements:

The teammates congratulated *themselves* on their victory.
She made a promise to *herself.*
The boss is not *himself* today.

b. They are called intensive when used as appositives, for emphasis:

I *myself* am to blame. Only they *themselves* are to blame.

Do not use a *-self* pronoun where a personal pronoun suffices:

WRONG: John and *myself* went.
RIGHT: John and *I* went.

NOTE: There are no such words in standard English as *hisself, ourself, ourselfs, theirself, theirselves, yourselfs, themself, themselfs.*

Use the Right Pronoun Case.

The case of a pronoun is the form it takes in a certain use in a sentence, such as subject or direct object. English has three cases: **nominative, possessive,** and **objective.** The pronouns with different nominative and objective forms cause the most confusion: *I/me, he/him, she/her, we/us, they/them, who/whom.*

Nominative Case (subject forms)	Possessive Case (possessive forms)	Objective Case (object forms)
SINGULAR		
I	my, mine	me
he, she, it	his, her, hers, its	him, her, it
PLURAL		
we	our, ours	us
they	their, theirs	them
SINGULAR OR PLURAL		
you	your, yours	you
who	whose	whom

6. NOMINATIVE CASE. Use the distinctive nominative (subject) forms—*I, he, she, we, they, who*—as

a. Subject: *I* know it. *She* and *I* know it. *Who* knows it?

b. Subjective complement (after linking verbs): The murderer is *she.*

NOTE: Although informal usage permits *It was her* or *It wasn't me,* most writers and speakers adhere to the nominative in formal usage: It was *she.* It was not *I.* See 8e below for pronoun case with the infinitive *to be.*

7. OBJECTIVE CASE. Use the distinctive objective (object) forms—*me, him, her, us, them, whom*—for any kind of object:

DIRECT OBJECT: We all greeted *him.*
INDIRECT OBJECT: We all gave *him* a present.
OBJECT OF PREPOSITION: We all gave a present to *him.*

8. SPECIAL PROBLEMS WITH NOMINATIVE AND OBJECTIVE CASES.

a. A pronoun in an *and* or *or* compound takes the same case as it would if the other part of the compound were not there:

WRONG: *Him* and *me* can go. [Would you say *Him can go* or *Me can go*?]
RIGHT: *He* and *I* can go. [*He* can go. *I* can go.]
WRONG: This gift is from Sally and *I.* [from *I*?]
RIGHT: This gift is from Sally and *me.* [from *me*]

b. A pronoun followed by a noun appositive takes the same case as it would if the noun were not there:

WRONG: *Us* girls want to thank you. [*Us* want . . .?]
RIGHT: *We* girls would like to thank you. [*We* want . . .]
RIGHT: He did it for *us* girls. [He did it for *us.*]

c. A pronoun appositive takes the same case as the word it is in apposition with:

Two *people, you* and *she,* will go.
Father took *us*—Jean and *me*—downtown.
Let's [Let *us*] *you* and *me* go to the store.

d. A pronoun in an incomplete comparison takes the same case it would if the comparison were complete:

RIGHT: She found Sid sooner than *I* [did].
RIGHT: She found Sid sooner than [she found] *me.*

Both of these sentences are correct, but each has a different meaning.

e. A pronoun between a verb and an infinitive (called the **subject of the infinitive**) takes the objective case:

I asked *him* to sing. We wanted *them* to stay.

NOTE: If the infinitive *to be* has such a subject, any pronoun following *to be* also takes the objective case (since *be* takes the same case after it as before it): *They thought her to be me. We wanted the winner to be him.* If *to be* does not have such a subject, any pronoun following *to be* takes the same case as the subject of the sentence (nominative): *The winner was thought to be she.*

9. POSSESSIVE CASE.

a. Use the apostrophe ['] to form the possessive case of indefinite and reciprocal pronouns: *someone's, everybody's, each other's, no one's,* etc.

b. Use the possessive case before a gerund:

WRONG: We resented *him* leaving.
RIGHT: We resented *his* leaving.

c. Do not use the apostrophe in the possessive case of personal pronouns (*his, hers, its, ours, yours, theirs*) or of *who* (*whose*):

Whose book is this? Is it *ours* or *theirs*? It can't be *hers.* It is a common error to confuse the possessives *its, whose, their,* and *your* with the contractions *it's* (*it is*), *who's* (*who is*), *they're* (*they are*) and *you're* (*you are*). Remember that no possessive personal pronoun ever takes an apostrophe, nor does *whose*:

The dog wagged *its* tail. *Whose* dog is that?
The dogs wagged *their* tails. Is that *your* dog?

NOTE: To tell which form you need, mentally substitute the uncontracted form (*it is,* etc.). If it sounds right, then you need the contraction:

(*Its/It's*) a fine day.→*It is* a fine day.→*It's* a fine day.
The tree shed (*its/it's*) leaves.→The tree shed *it is* leaves? No.→The tree shed *its* leaves.

10. THE CASE OF THE INTERROGATIVE PRONOUNS *who* and *whom*. *Who* is nominative case; *whom* is objective:

Who came in first? [subject]
Whom did you meet?→You did meet *whom*? [direct object]
Whom did you go with?→You did go with *whom*? [object of preposition]

NOTE: When in doubt about using *who* or *whom*, try substituting *he* or *him*. If *he* sounds right, use *who*; if *him* sounds right, use *whom*:

(*Who/Whom*) rang the bell?→*He* rang the bell?→*Who* rang the bell?
(*Who/Whom*) did you see?→You did see *him*?→You did see *whom*?→*Whom* did you see?

Although informal usage permits *Who did you see?* and *Who did you go with?* most careful writers adhere to *whom* in formal usage. Directly after a preposition, always use *whom*: With *whom* did you go?

11. THE CASE OF A RELATIVE PRONOUN is determined by its use *within* its clause:

She is the one *who scored the goal*. [*Who* = subject of *scored*.]
She is the one *whom they must stop*. [*They must stop whom*. *Whom* = direct object of *must stop*.]
You must tell *whoever comes*. [*Whoever* = subject of *comes*.]
You must tell *whomever you meet*. [*Whomever* = direct object of *meet*.]

Do not be misled by other intervening clauses, such as *I think*, *it seems*, or *we are convinced*:

She is the one *who* I think *scored the goal*.
She is the one *whom* it is certain *we must stop*.

Avoid Faulty Reference.

Be sure that each pronoun refers unmistakably only to its antecedent—the noun it stands for.

12. AMBIGUOUS REFERENCE occurs when a pronoun may refer to more than one noun. Clarify such ambiguity by rephrasing the sentence:

WRONG: Ms. Schatz has given the job to Ida because *she* knows what must be done. [Does *she* refer to Ms. Schatz or to Ida?]
RIGHT: Ms. Schatz, *who* knows what must be done, has given Ida the job.
RIGHT: Ms. Schatz has given the job to Ida, *who* knows what must be done.

13. VAGUE REFERENCE occurs when a pronoun has no easily identifiable antecedent. Clarify the sentence by supplying the needed noun:

WRONG: In England *they* drive on the left. [Who are *they*?]
RIGHT: The *English* drive on the left.

Avoid using *which*, *it*, *this*, or *that* to refer vaguely to a whole clause or sentence:

WRONG: The man had deliberately stepped on his toe, *which* bothered him. [Can you find a clear antecedent of *which*?]
RIGHT: The man's deliberate *stepping* on his toe bothered him.
RIGHT: The man had deliberately stepped on his toe, *an act that* bothered him.

It is acceptable in *It is raining*, *It is a fine day*, etc.

G-7. Recognizing Phrases

Being able to recognize phrases (and clauses) helps you avoid agreement errors, fragments, comma splices and fused sentences, and misplaced or dangling modifiers.

A **phrase** is a group of related words that is less complete than a sentence because it lacks subject + verb. (Some phrases contain a part of a verb—a verbal.) A phrase usually functions as if it were a single word: noun, adjective, or adverb. For this reason it is important to think of and recognize phrases as units. There are two main kinds of phrases:

1. THE PREPOSITIONAL PHRASE is used chiefly as adjective or adverb. It consists of preposition + object (and possible modifiers of that object):

AS ADJECTIVE: The house *with the red shutters* is ours. [tells which house]
AS ADVERB: She died *in the old hospital*. [tells where]
The boys did it *for a joke*. [tells why]

2. THE VERBAL PHRASE. There are three kinds: infinitive, gerund, and participial. (See G-4.6, page 4, for explanation of these terms.)

a. An infinitive phrase (infinitive + complement or modifiers or both):

AS NOUN: *To become premier* is her aim. [subject]
She wants *to become premier*. [direct object]
AS ADJECTIVE: I have a plan *to suggest to you*. [modifies *plan*]
AS ADVERB: We ventured forth *to meet the foe*. [modifies *ventured*]
Oscar is eager *to leave soon*. [modifies *eager*]

b. A participial phrase (a present or past participle + complement or modifiers or both). It is always used as an adjective:

The young man *reading a trashy novel* is my son. [modifies *man*]
Immersed in a trashy novel, the young man ignored his mother. [modifies *man*]

Another kind of phrase using a participle is the **absolute phrase** (subject + participle + complement or modifiers or both), so called because it is grammatically independent of the sentence (though logically connected to it):

Her face reddening, Karen muttered an apology.
Karen muttered an apology, *her face reddening*.

c. A gerund phrase (*-ing* form + complement or modifiers or both). It is always used as a noun:

Reading a trashy novel is a waste of time. [subject]
How can you enjoy *reading a trashy novel*? [direct object]
His chief pastime is *reading a trashy novel*. [subjective complement]
He relaxes by *reading a trashy novel*. [object of preposition]

For avoidance of dangling or misplaced phrases, see G-10.8–9, page 10.

NOTE: Some authorities use the term **noun phrase** to refer to a noun + its modifiers (*the five old men in their wheelchairs*), and **verb phrase** for a main verb and its auxiliaries (*might have been drinking*).

G-8. Recognizing Clauses

A **clause** is a group of related words containing subject + verb. There are two kinds: **independent** (**main**) and **dependent** (**subordinate**).

1. AN INDEPENDENT CLAUSE sounds complete and makes sense when it stands alone. Every simple sentence is an independent clause; however, the term *clause* usually refers to such a word group as part of a larger sentence:

I found the key, and *I gave it to Helen*.

2. A DEPENDENT CLAUSE, though it contains subject + verb, cannot stand alone grammatically. What makes a clause dependent is a connecting word that forces the clause to be linked to an independent clause:

[dependent clause in italics; connecting word in bold]

We will cheer **when** *the Canadian astronaut returns*.
I recognized the scarf **that** *she was wearing*.

Dependent Clauses Are Used as Three Parts of Speech.

3. AN ADJECTIVE CLAUSE functions as an adjective, modifying a noun or pronoun. It is introduced and connected to the independent clause by the relative pronoun *who* (*whose*, *whom*), *which*, or *that*, or sometimes by *when*, *where*, or *why*:

The boy *who applied for work* was hired. [modifies *boy*]
We greeted everyone *who came.* [modifies *everyone*]
Let's see King Kong, *which is playing downtown.* [modifies *King Kong*]
Give this to the person *that collects the tickets.* [modifies *person*]

Adjective clauses are either **restrictive** or **nonrestrictive**, depending on their necessity in the sentence. See P-1.5b, page 13, for explanation and punctuation.

4. AN ADVERB CLAUSE functions as an adverb, modifying a verb, adjective, or other adverb. It tells *how, when, where, to what degree, why,* or *under what condition.* It is introduced and connected to the independent clause by one of the subordinate conjunctions listed below:

ADVERB CLAUSE TELLING	INTRODUCED BY SUBORDINATE CONJUNCTION	EXAMPLE
Time [*when?*]	when(ever), while, after, before, since, as, as soon as	I left *before Jo returned.*
Place [*where?*]	where, wherever	We went *where the land was fertile.*
Manner [*how?*]	as, as if, as though	He walks *as if he's dazed.*
Clause [*why?*]	because, since	I left *because I was angry.*
Purpose [*why?*]	(so) that, in order that	She came *so that she might help.*
Concession [*under what condition?*]	(al)though, even though	They came, *although they were tired.*
Condition [*under what condition?*]	if, unless, whether, provided	You can go *if you leave early.*
Result [*that what resulted?*]	that	He ran so fast *that he was exhausted.*
Comparison [*to what degree?*]	as, than	She is taller *than I [am].*

Most adverb clauses can appear at the beginning of a sentence:
If you leave early, you can go.

5. A NOUN CLAUSE functions as a noun. It is introduced and connected to the independent clause by the relative pronoun *who(ever), which(ever), what(ever),* or *that* or by *when, where, why, how,* or *whether*:
What they did made little sense. [subject]
I know *that he went.* [direct object]
Give *whoever answers the door* this note. [indirect object]
Give this note to *whoever answers the door.* [object of preposition]

6. CLAUSES IN SENTENCES. Sentences can be classified according to their structure, that is, the number and kind(s) of clauses they have. There are four kinds of sentences:

a. The simple sentence (one independent clause):
The door opened.

b. The compound sentence (two or more independent clauses):
The door opened, and *our guests entered.*
The clock struck eight, the door opened, and *our guests entered.*

c. The complex sentence (one independent clause and one or more dependent clauses):
[dependent clause in bold]
As the clock struck eight, *the door opened.*

d. The compound-complex sentence (a compound sentence + one or more dependent clauses):
As the clock struck eight, *the door opened* and *our guests entered.*

G-9. Agreement

Agreement means that a verb must match its subject in grammatical form and that a pronoun must match its antecedent in grammatical form. Grammatical form includes person and number.

Make Every Verb Agree with Its Subject in Person and number.

1. THERE ARE THREE GRAMMATICAL PERSONS: the **first person** [the person(s) speaking: *I, we*], the **second person** [the person(s) being spoken to: *you*], and the **third person** [the person(s) being spoken about: *he, she, it, they,* and any noun]. In most verbs, only the third person present tense singular has a special form: the ending *-s. I run, we run,* and *you run,* but *he* or *she runs.* The verb *be* is special. The first person is *I am, we are* (past tense: *I was, we were*); the second person is *you are* (past tense: *you were*); the third person is *he* or *she is, they are* (past tense: *he* or *she was, they were*). Use the verb form that matches the person of the subject:

WRONG: You is late.   RIGHT: You are late.
2d PERSON   3d PERSON   2d PERSON   2d PERSON

NOTE: When two or more subjects in different persons are joined by *or,* the verb agrees with the subject nearer to it:
Either she or I *am* going.

2. THERE ARE TWO GRAMMATICAL NUMBERS: singular (referring to one thing) and **plural** (referring to more than one). Singular subjects must take singular verbs; plural subjects must take plural verbs. Except for *be* (see 1 above), only the third person singular in the present and present perfect tenses presents a problem, because of its *-s* ending.

[singular in bold; plural in italics]
WRONG: **Jo** *like* chips. **She** *don't* [*do not*] like pizza.
RIGHT: **Jo likes** chips. **She doesn't** [**does not**] like pizza.

3. INTERVENING WORD GROUPS. Make subject and verb agree regardless of phrases or clauses that come between them:
PHRASE: The *collection* (of rare books) *is* lost.
CLAUSE: The *woman* (who owns these horses) *lives* here.

Parenthetical phrases introduced by *(together) with, like, as well as, including, in addition to,* etc., do not affect the number of the actual subject:
Elizabeth, together with her friends, *is* coming.
The *boys,* as well as their father, *have* arrived.

4. TWO OR MORE SUBJECTS.

a. Joined by *and*. Use a plural verb with two or more subjects joined by *and*:
A *book* and a *pencil are* all I need.
Are chemistry and history *required?*

However, if both subjects refer to a single person or thing, use a singular verb:
My *friend and benefactor is* here. [One person is both friend and benefactor.]
Scotch and soda is my favorite drink. [one drink]

Use a singular verb when *each* or *every* precedes the subjects:
Every man and every woman is expected to pay.

b. Joined by *or* or *nor*. Use a singular verb with two or more singular subjects joined by *or* or *nor*:
Bettina or Sharon is going with you.

Use a plural verb when both subjects are plural:
The *Canadiens* or the *Nordiques are* going to finish first.

When one subject is singular and the other plural, make the verb agree with the nearer subject:

Bettina or the *twins* *are going* with you.
The *twins* or *Bettina* *is going* with you.

5. SINGULAR PRONOUNS. Use a singular verb when the subject is the singular indefinite pronoun *one*, *each*, *either*, *neither*, *everyone*, *everybody*, *anyone*, *anybody*, *someone*, *somebody*, *no one*, or *nobody*:

Each of them *wants* me to stay.
Everyone is going home.

After *all*, *any*, *most*, *none*, *some*, or *such*, use either a singular or a plural verb, depending on whether the pronoun refers to something singular or plural:

The milk was left in the sun; *all* of it *has turned* sour.
The guests became bored; *all have left.*
Such were the joys of youth. *Such is* the way of the world.

6. COLLECTIVE NOUNS. Use a singular verb when thinking of the group as a unit:

A new *family has moved* next door.

Use a plural verb when thinking of the group members as individuals:

The new *family have been fighting* with one another.

7. LINKING VERBS. Make a linking verb agree with its subject, not its subjective complement:

Books are her chief interest. Her chief *interest is* books.

8. SINGULAR NOUNS IN PLURAL FORM. Such nouns as *news*, *billiards*, *whereabouts*, *athletics*, *measles*, *mumps*, *mathematics*, and *economics* are logically singular. Use a singular verb:

Her *whereabouts is* unknown.
Measles has been nearly *eliminated.*

However, use a plural verb with two-part things such as *trousers*, *pants*, *pliers*, *scissors*, *tweezers*:

The *tweezers are* not useful for this; perhaps the *pliers are.*

9. *It* AND *there* AS EXPLETIVES (words with no meaning in a sentence).

  a. *There* is never the subject. In sentences beginning with *there is (was)* or *there are (were)*, look *after* the verb for the subject, and make the verb agree with the subject:

There *is* a *bee* in your bonnet. [A *bee is* in your bonnet.]
There *are bats* in your belfry. [*Bats are* in your belfry.]

  b. *It*, on the other hand, is always singular:

It was Uncle Wayne who telephoned.
It was the boys who telephoned.

10. LITERARY TITLES AND WORDS CONSIDERED AS WORDS ARE ALWAYS SINGULAR.
The Diviners is not a light novel.
Children is an irregular plural.

11. SUMS OF MONEY AND MEASUREMENTS. When considering a sum as a single item, use a singular verb:

Ten dollars is not much money these days.
Five gallons is the capacity of this tank.

When considering individual dollars, gallons, miles, etc., use a plural verb:

The *dollars were* neatly *arranged* in stacks.
Gallons of gasoline *are spilling* from the tank.

In an arithmetic problem, you may use either:

Six and four is [*makes*] ten. *Six and four are* [*make*] ten.
NOTE: The number takes a singular verb; *a number*, plural.

12. RELATIVE PRONOUNS. After *who*, *which*, or *that*, use a singular verb if the pronoun's antecedent is singular, a plural verb if its antecedent is plural:

She is the only *member who smokes.* [Antecedent of *who* is *member.*]
She is one of the *members who smoke.* [Antecedent of *who* is *members.*]
It is *I who am* responsible. [Antecedent of *who* is *I.*]

Make Every Pronoun Agree with Its Antecedent in Person and Number.

13. AVOID ILLOGICAL SHIFTS TO *you*.
  WRONG: *I* like swimming because it gives *you* firm muscles.
  RIGHT: *I* like swimming because it gives *me* firm muscles.
  WRONG: If *a person* eats just before swimming, *you* may get a cramp.
  RIGHT: If *a person* eats just before swimming, *he* may get a cramp.

14. SINGULAR PRONOUNS. Use a singular pronoun when referring to antecedents such as *person*, *man*, *woman*, *one*, *anyone*, *anybody*, *someone*, *somebody*, *either*, *neither*, *each*, *everyone*, *everybody*:

A *person* should know what *he* wants in life.
Neither of the women will state *her* preference.

NOTE: When a singular antecedent may be either masculine or feminine (such as *student*, *citizen*), you have three choices:

  (1) Use the masculine pronoun: Every *student* raised *his* hand.
  (2) Use both pronouns: Every *student* raised *his or her* hand.
  (3) Change the sentence to plural: The *students* raised *their* hands.

Many people consider choice 1 sexist and choice 2 awkward; when it is possible and not inconsistent with surrounding sentences, choice 3 is probably best.

15. ANTECEDENTS JOINED BY *and*, *or*, AND *nor*. Follow the same principles as for subject-verb agreement (see 4 above).

  a. For antecedents joined by *and*, use a plural pronoun:

Bettina and *Sharon* are performing *their* act.

  b. For antecedents joined by *or* or *nor*, use a singular pronoun if the antecedents are singular, plural if they are plural:

Either *Bettina* or *Sharon* will perform *her* act.
The *Canadiens* or the *Nordiques* should win *their* divisional title.

For one singular and one plural antecedent, make the pronoun agree with the nearer antecedent:

Either *Bettina* or the *twins* will perform *their* act.

16. COLLECTIVE NOUNS. Follow the same principle as for subject-verb agreement (see 6 above); let the meaning of the noun determine the number of the pronoun:

The *family* has moved into *its* new home.
The *family* have settled *their* differences.

17. DEMONSTRATIVE PRONOUNS USED AS ADJECTIVES. Make *this*, *that*, *these*, or *those* agree with the noun it modifies:

  WRONG: I like *these kind* of fish. [*These* is plural; *kind*, singular.]
  RIGHT: I like *this kind* of fish. I like *these kinds* of fish.

G-10. Effective Sentences

Good sentences reflect clear thinking. A clumsy sentence says that an idea has been poorly thought out. Consider, therefore, not only what you want to say but how you can best say it. A well-written sentence has **unity**, **coherence**, and **emphasis**. Unity and coherence make it logical and clear; emphasis makes it forceful.

Use the Following Guidelines to Write More Effective Sentences.

  1. AVOID OVERUSE OF SHORT, CHOPPY SENTENCES. A short, simple sentence can be forceful: *The king is dead.* But a long string of short sentences usually gives a childish effect: *I walked through the woods. I saw a squirrel. It darted up a tree.* Usually you can combine related ideas in a way that shows your reader their relation and their relative importance. The following sections 2–4 describe some combining techniques.

2. USE COORDINATION. You can regard related simple sentences as independent clauses and join them with a co-ordinate conjunction (preceded by a comma) to form a compound sentence:

WEAK: The princess had many suitors. She cared for none.

BETTER: The princess had many suitors, *but* she cared for none. [The conjunction *but* shows the contrast between the two facts.]

WEAK: We walked to work. The day was sunny.

BETTER: We walked to work, *for* the day was sunny. [The conjunction *for* shows that one fact caused the other.]

WEAK: Mullins had been tricked once. He didn't want to be tricked again.

BETTER: Mullins had been tricked once, *and* he didn't want to be tricked again. [The *and* adds little meaning, but the one longer sentence reads more smoothly than the two shorter ones.]

NOTE: Although joining equally important clauses with coordinate conjunctions can be effective, using too many *and*'s or *so*'s offers little if any improvement over the string of short simple sentences you are trying to avoid. As alternatives, consider compounding and subordination, below.

3. USE COMPOUNDING. Combine simple sentences that have the same subjects or verbs so that you have only one sentence, with a compound subject or predicate:

WEAK: Carol is learning tennis. I am learning tennis too.

BETTER: [*Both*] *Carol and I* are learning tennis.

NOTE: Check subject-verb agreement as you rewrite using compounding.

WEAK: We put up the tent. We fell asleep at once.

BETTER: We *put* up the tent *and fell* asleep at once.

NOTE: Ordinarily there is no comma between the parts of a compound predicate.

4. USE SUBORDINATION. You can give one idea less emphasis by making it into a dependent clause. By doing so you usually express the relation between ideas more clearly than by coordination or compounding:

WEAK: The sun came out. Sally headed for the beach.

BETTER: *When* the sun came out, Sally headed for the beach. [*When* stresses the time connection between the two facts.]

BETTER: *Because* the sun came out, Sally headed for the beach. [*Because* stresses the causal connection between the two facts.]

BETTER: Sally, *who* was glad to see the sun come out, headed for the beach. [The idea in the *who* clause is reduced to secondary importance.]

Be careful not to subordinate the *main* idea—the one you would mention if you could mention only one:

WRONG: President Kennedy, *who was shot dead*, was riding in an open car.

RIGHT: *President Kennedy*, who was riding in an open car, *was shot dead*.

5. USE REDUCTION. Whenever possible, eliminate needless words by reducing clauses to phrases and phrases to single words:

WORDY (CLAUSE): *Because she was discouraged about writing stories*, Erika decided to try nonfiction.

TIGHTER (PHRASE): *Discouraged about writing stories*, Erika decided to try nonfiction.

WORDY (CLAUSE): The person *who is holding the pistol* is the starter.

TIGHTER (PHRASE): The person *holding the pistol* is the starter.

WORDY (PHRASE): That woman *with the blonde hair* is my professor.

TIGHTER (WORD): That *blonde* woman is my professor.

NOTE: Use caution in placing modifiers; see 8 and 9 below.

6. USE PARALLEL STRUCTURE (the same grammatical form) with two or more coordinate expressions, in comparisons, and with correlative conjunctions:

WRONG: Kay is *vivacious* [adjective], *with keen wit* [prepositional phrase], and *has a friendly manner* [verb + complement].

RIGHT: Kay is *vivacious, keen-witted*, and *friendly* [all adjectives].

WRONG: Arthur likes *drinking* and *to gamble*.

RIGHT: Arthur likes *drinking* and *gambling* [or *to drink* and *to gamble*].

WRONG: Arthur likes *gambling* more than *to drink*.

RIGHT: Arthur likes *gambling* more than *drinking*.

WRONG: Jo **not only** *likes* [verb] dogs **but also** *cats* [noun].

RIGHT: Jo likes **not only** *dogs* [noun] **but also** *cats* [noun].

Avoid These Faults in Sentence Construction:

7. FRAGMENTS; COMMA SPLICES AND FUSED SENTENCES (RUN–ONS). See G-1.5, page 1, and P-1.19, page 13.

8. NEEDLESS SEPARATION OF RELATED PARTS OF A SENTENCE.

a. Do not needlessly separate subject and verb or verb and complement:

WRONG: *I*, hoping very much to see him, *hurried*.

RIGHT: Hoping very much to see him, *I hurried*.

b. Place modifying words, phrases, and clauses next to the words they modify:

Adverb:

WRONG: What great luck! I *almost* won $1,000 in the lottery. [*Almost won* means that you came close but did not win anything.]

RIGHT: What luck! I won *almost* **$1,000** in the lottery.

Only, *nearly*, *scarcely*, *hardly*, *just*, and *even* present the same problem.

Phrase:

WRONG: Notify us if you can **come** *on the enclosed card*.

RIGHT: **Notify** us *on the enclosed card* if you can come. [*On the enclosed card* should modify *notify*, not *come*.]

WRONG: *Floating inside the bottle*, **Ms. Fleisch** saw some mysterious specks.

RIGHT: Ms. Fleisch saw some mysterious **specks** *floating inside the bottle*.

Clause:

WRONG: Ann put a hat on her **head** *that she had just bought*.

RIGHT: On her head Ann put a **hat** *that she had just bought*.

c. Avoid "squinting" modifiers: A squinter comes between two verbs so that the reader cannot tell which verb it refers to:

WRONG: Mark **decided** *after his vacation* to **see** a doctor.

RIGHT: Mark decided to **see** a doctor *after his vacation*.

RIGHT: *After his vacation*, Mark **decided** to see a doctor.

d. Avoid awkward splitting of infinitives: The two parts of an infinitive belong together; avoid putting words between them unless your sentence would otherwise be unclear or sound odd:

POOR: I asked her *to from time to time visit* me.

BETTER: I asked her *to visit* me from time to time.

e. In formal English, avoid ending a sentence with a preposition unless the sentence would otherwise sound awkward:

INFORMAL: Sculpture is one art [*which*] she excelled *at*.

FORMAL: Sculpture is one art *at which* she excelled.

9. DANGLING MODIFIERS. A modifier (usually a phrase) "dangles" when there is no word in the sentence that it can sensibly modify. Correct a dangler in either of two ways shown below.

a. Dangling participle:

WRONG: *Flying over Switzerland*, the jagged **Alps** appeared awesome. [The nearest noun to the phrase should name the persons doing the flying. Instead, the sentence seems to say that the Alps were flying.]

RIGHT: *Flying over Switzerland*, **we** were awed by the jagged Alps. [right noun put nearest to phrase]

RIGHT: *As we flew over Switzerland*, the jagged Alps appeared awesome. [phrase expanded into a clause]

b. Dangling gerund:

WRONG: *After walking for hours*, the **cabin** appeared around a bend.

RIGHT: *After walking for hours*, the **hikers** saw the cabin appear around a bend.

RIGHT: *After the hikers had walked for hours*, the cabin appeared around a bend.

c. Dangling infinitive:

WRONG: *To be well cooked*, **you** must boil the beets for half an hour.

RIGHT: *To be well cooked*, **beets** must be boiled for half an hour.

d. Dangling elliptical clause: An elliptical clause is one from which the subject and all or part of the verb have been dropped as understood, e.g., *while* [I was] *skiing in Utah.*

WRONG: *While still a toddler*, my **father** gave me swimming lessons.

RIGHT: *While I was still a toddler*, my father gave me swimming lessons.

RIGHT: *While still a toddler*, **I** was given swimming lessons by my father.

Ellipsis is permissible only when the subject of both clauses is the same, as in the last example above (*I* is the understood subject of the elliptical clause).

10. OMITTED NECESSARY WORDS IN A COMPARISON OR STATEMENT OF DEGREE.

WRONG: I felt *so* sad.

RIGHT: I felt *so* sad *that I cried.*

WRONG: Salaries of airline executives are higher *than* pilots.

RIGHT: Salaries of airline executives are higher *than those of* pilots.

11. NEEDLESS SHIFTS.

a. In number:

WRONG: If *a person* works hard, *they* will succeed.

RIGHT: If *a person* works hard, *he* will succeed.

RIGHT: If *people* work hard, *they* will succeed.

This is a matter of agreement; see G-9.14, page 9.

b. In person:

WRONG: If *a person* works hard, *you* will succeed.

See the correct sentences in *a* above. Also see G-9.13, page 9.

c. In subject or voice of verb:

WRONG: As *we approached* the house, *laughter could be heard*. [*Approached* is active; *could be heard*, passive. Subject shifts from *we* to *laughter*.]

RIGHT: As *we approached* the house, *we could hear* laughter.

d. In tense of verb: See G-4.7, page 4.

e. In mood of verb:

WRONG: *Finish* your work, and then you *should rest.* [*Finish* is imperative in mood; *should rest*, indicative.]

RIGHT: *Finish* your work, and then *rest.*

12. REDUNDANT OR INFLATED WORDING.

a. Redundancy (needless repetition) in general:

WRONG: *In* this book *it* states that we have an *absolutely* unique town hall. *This town hall* is the tallest *in height* in the nation. *In my opinion, I think* that we should be proud of that.

RIGHT: This book states that we have a unique town hall, the tallest in the nation. We should be proud of that.

b. Double negatives:

WRONG: I *can't hardly* hear you. [*Hardly, barely*, and *scarcely* mean *almost not*, and thus act as negatives.]

RIGHT: I *can hardly* hear you. I *can't* hear you.

c. Superfluous *that:*

WRONG: We know *that*, although we won, *that* we won't get the prize.

RIGHT: We know *that*, although we won, we won't get the prize.

d. Inflated phrasing: Avoid excessive use of elaborate modifiers and Latinate diction (words with endings such as *-tion* or *-ify*) to make your writing sound more impressive. It is better to express ideas in simple, direct language. By all means, try to increase your vocabulary, but use words with accuracy and intent to convey meaning, not merely to impress your reader. Otherwise, your writing may appear affected, and you may even obscure your ideas:

INFLATED: Individuals who have undergone the training process in emergency rescue procedures have on numerous occasions demonstrated the ability to implement such techniques in the prevention of fatalities within their own family units.

BETTER: People trained in emergency rescuing have often been able to save lives in accidents in their own homes.

Punctuation

Most punctuation marks represent the pauses and stops we would use in speaking. Periods, question marks, exclamation points, semicolons, and colons are stop marks—the "red lights" of writing. Commas and dashes are pause marks—the "amber lights" that tell us to slow down momentarily. Some punctuation marks *separate* words and ideas; others *group* and *keep together* related ideas; still others *set aside* words for special emphasis. In all, they clarify written material that would otherwise be confusing and at times misleading.

Most punctuation rules are not difficult to master. Careful writers learn these rules and tend to conform to the established pattern of punctuation, reserving their originality not for devising their own mode of punctuation but for choosing and arranging the words with which they present their ideas to the reader.

P-1. The Comma [,]

Since misuse of the comma accounts for about half of all punctuation errors, carefully studying these rules should enable you to punctuate more clearly and effectively.

Use the Comma to Set Off

1. INDEPENDENT (MAIN) CLAUSES. A comma follows the first of two independent clauses that are joined by coordinate conjunctions (*and*, *but*, *or*, *nor*, *for*, *yet*):

> The play's star is Richard Monnette, *and* its author is Michel Tremblay.
> Tremblay's early plays were performed only in Quebec, but his more recent ones have been staged across Canada.

NOTE: In informal writing, *so* is sometimes used as a coordinate conjunction; however, in formal writing this use of *so* is generally avoided.

Do *not* use a comma

a. If there is no full clause (subject + verb) after the conjunction:

WRONG: George straightened his tie, *and* put on his jacket.
RIGHT: George straightened his tie *and* put on his jacket.

b. *After* the conjunction:
WRONG: I ordered chicken *but*, he ordered lobster.
RIGHT: I ordered chicken, *but* he ordered lobster.

c. Between very short independent clauses:

He lies and she cheats.

d. Between independent clauses not joined by a coordinate conjunction (use a semicolon instead):

WRONG: The starting gun sounded, the crowd roared.
RIGHT: The starting gun sounded; the crowd roared.

See comma splice and fused sentence, P-1.19, page 13.

2. INTRODUCTORY ELEMENTS.

a. An introductory adverb clause:

If you pay full tuition now, you can register by mail.

NOTE: Usually you need no comma when the adverb clause is at the end of the sentence: You can register by mail *if you pay full tuition now*.

b. A long prepositional phrase or a series of prepositional phrases:

In the cool air of that April morning, we strolled along the boulevard.

NOTE: Unless clarity demands one, you do not need a comma after one short introductory phrase: *In the morning* we strolled along the boulevard.

c. A verbal phrase:

Speaking off the record, the mayor admitted the error.
To play bridge well, you need a good memory.
By *playing bridge every week*, Stella sharpened her mind.

An infinitive or gerund phrase used as the *subject* of a sentence is not an introductory element. Do not set it off:

To play bridge well is my ambition.
Playing bridge every week sharpened Stella's mind.

3. ITEMS IN A SERIES. Use commas to separate words, phrases, or clauses in a series of three or more:

WORDS: I enjoy the old films of *Bogart*, *Cagney*, *Garbo*, and *Hepburn*.
PHRASES: The book is available *in bookstores*, *at newsstands*, or *by mail*.
CLAUSES: *She took French lessons*, *she studied guide books*, and *she talked to people who had been to Paris*.

NOTE: Some writers omit the comma before *and* or *or* in a series. Including this comma, however, ensures clarity:

POSSIBLY CONFUSING: Edmund bought spaghetti, pancake mix, *pork and beans*. [Did he buy pork and beans separately or one can of pork and beans?]
CLEAR: Edmund bought spaghetti, pancake mix, *pork*, and *beans*.
CLEAR: Edmund bought spaghetti, pancake mix, and *pork and beans*.

Always use a comma before *etc.* at the end of a series: pork, beans, *etc.*

Do *not* use a comma

a. With only two items: Edmund bought *spaghetti* and *pork*.

b. When you repeat *and* or *or* between every two items: Edmund bought spaghetti *and* pancake mix *and* pork.

c. Before the first item or after the last item:

WRONG: Edmund *bought*, *spaghetti*, pancake mix, and pork.
RIGHT: Edmund *bought spaghetti*, pancake mix, and pork.
WRONG: Spaghetti, pancakes, and *pork*, *are* not everyone's favorites.
RIGHT: Spaghetti, pancakes, and *pork are* not everyone's favorites.

4. COORDINATE ADJECTIVES. In a series of two or more, use commas to separate adjectives of equal importance. Do not put a comma after the last adjective:

Tall, *stately* trees lined the roadway.
Vulgar, *snide*, or *obscene* remarks are not appreciated here.

NOTE: Certain combinations of adjectives flow naturally together and need no commas: *little red* schoolhouse; *five funny old* men; *additional monetary* demands. Determining when to omit commas is tricky, but generally, if the adjectives sound odd in a different order (*red little* schoolhouse, *old funny five* men, *monetary additional* demands), you probably should omit commas.

5. PARENTHETICAL EXPRESSIONS. These are words or word groups that interrupt the main flow of thought in a sentence and are not essential to the meaning of the sentence.

a. General parenthetical expressions:

She was, *in my opinion*, outstanding.
He, *on the other hand*, performed unconvincingly.
The entire production, *moreover*, lacked vitality.

It is unfortunate, *to be sure.* [Note the vast difference in meaning from *It is unfortunate to be sure.*]

Other common parenthetical expressions include *as a matter of fact*, *to tell the truth*, *of course*, *incidentally*, *namely*, *in the first place*, *therefore*, *thus*, *consequently*, *however*, *nevertheless*.

NOTE: Not all these expressions are always set off. You may choose not to set off *also*, *too*, *perhaps*, *likewise*, *at least*, *indeed*, *therefore*, *thus*, and certain others in sentences where you feel they do not interrupt your thought flow:

We may, *perhaps*, have been harsh in firing Jenkins.
We may *perhaps* have been harsh in firing Jenkins.

See P-5.2, page 15, for other punctuation with *therefore*, *however*, and other conjunctive adverbs.

b. Nonrestrictive (nonessential) clauses: A **nonrestrictive** clause (usually beginning with *which* or a form of *who*) is parenthetical. The information it gives is *not* essential to the meaning of the sentence. Being parenthetical, such a clause is set off within commas:

Parsons Boulevard, *which runs past my home*, is being repaved.
Penny Prentiss, *who lives in Hill Hall*, has won the award.

A **restrictive** clause *is* essential to the meaning of the sentence. It identifies a preceding noun; it answers the question "which one?" Such a clause is written without commas:

The street *which runs past my home* is being repaved.
A woman *who lives in Hill Hall* has won the award.

These restrictive clauses tell *which* street and *which* woman. Without the clauses the sentences could refer to any street or any woman. There is an easy test to distinguish restrictive from nonrestrictive clauses. A restrictive clause will sound right if you substitute *that* for *who* or *which*; a nonrestrictive clause will not.

SOUNDS RIGHT: A woman *that lives in Hill Hall* has won the award. [Test works; clause is restrictive. Omit commas.]
SOUNDS WRONG: Penny Prentiss *that lives in Hill Hall* has won the award. [Test fails; clause is nonrestrictive. Use commas (and *who*).]

c. Nonrestrictive (nonessential) phrases: Follow the principle for nonrestrictive clauses (see *b* above):

RESTRICTIVE: The woman *wearing red* is Jack's sister.
NONRESTRICTIVE: Ms. Atlee, *wearing red*, is Jack's sister.
RESTRICTIVE: The locker *with the Beatles poster* is mine.
NONRESTRICTIVE: Locker 356, *with the Beatles poster*, is mine.

d. Most appositives:

Canada's greatest novelist, Robertson Davies, was once a journalist.
The hermit crab, *a South Pacific species*, seals itself into its home for life.

NOTE: Some appositives are restrictive and take no commas:

The novelist *Robertson Davies* was once a journalist.
I wrote to my daughter *Ella*. [identifies which of several daughters]

6. ABSOLUTE PHRASES.

The day being warm, we headed for the beach.
Bosley, *his clothes hanging in tatters*, staggered into camp.

7. NAMES OR OTHER WORDS USED IN DIRECT ADDRESS.

Henry, what are you doing?
For my encore, *ladies and gentlemen*, I will play *Träumerei*.

8. YES AND *NO* AT THE BEGINNING OF A SENTENCE.

Yes, we have neckties on sale.

9. MILD INTERJECTIONS (expressions of less than strong emotion).

Well, I'll have to think that over.
Oh, what did she say?

NOTE: Strong interjections take exclamation points: *What!* I can't believe it.

10. DIRECT QUOTATIONS. Generally, use one or more commas to separate a direct quotation from explanatory words, such as *she said*:

"I love you," she whispered.
"And I," he replied, "love you."

NOTE: Punctuation of quotations is treated fully in P-8, page 16.

11. EXAMPLES INTRODUCED BY *such as*, *especially*, *particularly*; EXPRESSIONS OF CONTRAST.

Ira enjoys all crafts, *especially* wood carving.
On weekends we offer several courses, *such as* Biology 101 and Music 210.
Dresden lies in East Germany, *not* West Germany.

NOTE: Some *such as* phrases are restrictive: Days *such as* this are rare.

Use the Comma Also

12. IN PLACE OF OMITTED OR UNDERSTOOD WORDS.

Shirley attends McGill; *her brother*, Concordia.

13. BEFORE A CONFIRMATORY QUESTION.

It's a warm day, *isn't it?*

14. IN LETTERS.

a. After the greeting in a friendly letter: *Dear Mabel*,

NOTE: Use a colon after the greeting in a business letter: *Dear Ms. Worth*:

b. After the complimentary close in all letters: *Very truly yours,*

15. IN DATES AND ADDRESSES. In a month-day-year date, place the year within commas, as if it were parenthetical. Do the same with the state or country in an address:

On March 3, *1965*, I was born in Estivan, *Saskatchewan*, during a blizzard.

16. TO GROUP WORDS TO PREVENT MISREADING.

Inside, the dog was growling. [not *Inside the dog . . .*]
After eating, the child became sleepy. [not *After eating the child . . .*]

Do *Not* Use a Comma

17. TO SEPARATE SUBJECT AND VERB.

WRONG: Deciduous *trees*, *change* color in the fall.
RIGHT: Deciduous *trees change* color in the fall.

18. TO SEPARATE VERB AND COMPLEMENT.

WRONG: On vacation we *saw*, *countless lakes and hills*.
RIGHT: On vacation we *saw countless lakes and hills*.

19. TO JOIN TWO INDEPENDENT CLAUSES IN PLACE OF A COORDINATE CONJUNCTION (*and*, *but*, *or*, *nor*, *for*, *yet*).

WRONG: The day was stifling, it made me feel sluggish.
WRONG: The Oilers won decisively, they had superior coaching.

Writers of sentences such as these show a serious lack of understanding of what a complete sentence is. This kind of error is called a **comma splice** (or **comma fault** or **run-on**). Another, even worse kind of run-on is the **fused sentence**, in which the writer joins two independent clauses with no punctuation at all:

WRONG: The day was stifling it made me sluggish.

To avoid comma splices and fused sentences, first be sure that you can recognize an independent clause. Review G-8.1, page 7, if necessary. Next, learn these four ways to correct run-ons; choose the way that best fits your purpose and your paragraph.

a. Separate the clauses into two sentences:

RIGHT: The day was stifling. It made me sluggish.

This is the simplest but rarely the best way, for too many short sentences make your writing sound choppy and immature. Moreover, you fail to specify a relation between the ideas in the clauses.

b. Join the clauses with a coordinating conjunction:

RIGHT: The day was stifling, *and* it made me feel sluggish.

This is often a better way than making separate sentences, but you must not overuse this either. *And*, especially, shows only a very general relation between ideas.

c. Join the clauses with a semicolon:

RIGHT: The day was stifling; it made me sluggish.

A semicolon gives your writing a formal tone; it is often effective in balanced sentences, such as *Today was delightful; yesterday was dreadful*.

d. Join the clauses by making one of them a dependent (subordinate) clause: Join them with subordinate conjunctions, such as *because, if, when, since, after, although*, and *unless*, or with relative pronouns: *who(m), which, that*. Subordinating is often the best way to eliminate run-ons, since the kinds of words listed here show the precise relation between ideas:

RIGHT: I felt sluggish *because the day was stifling*.

RIGHT: The Oilers, *who had superior coaching*, won decisively. For more on subordination, see G-8.2–5, page 7, and G-10.4, page 10.

P-2. The Period [.]

Use a Period

1. AFTER EVERY SENTENCE EXCEPT A DIRECT QUESTION OR AN EXCLAMATION.

The index dropped six points. [declarative sentence]
Sell your stocks now. [imperative sentence]
I asked how I should sell them. [indirect question; the direct question would be *How shall I sell them*?]

2. AFTER AN ABBREVIATION OR INITIAL.

Mr., U.S., Dr., Ont., M.D., Rev., kg.

NOTE: Ms. takes a period. *Miss* does not.

Do *not* use a period with

a. Initials of many organizations that are well known by those initials: CN, RCMP, CBC, UN, YMCA

b. Radio and television stations: CHUM

c. Money in even-dollar denominations: $40 (but $40.99)

d. Contractions: ass'n, sec'y [for *association, secretary*. They may also be written *assn., secy.*]

e. Ordinal numbers: 5th, 2nd, Henry VIII

f. Nicknames: Rob, Pat, Sid, Pam

g. Common shortened terms: memo, math, exam, lab, gym, TV [All these terms are colloquial; use the full words in formal writing.]

3. AFTER A NUMBER OR LETTER IN A FORMAL OUTLINE.

I. Sports taught this semester
A. Swimming
B. Softball

NOTE: Do *not* use a period

a. If the number or letter is within parentheses: (1), (a)

b. If the number is part of a title: Chapter 4, Henry V

4. IN A GROUP OF THREE (...) TO SHOW THE FOLLOWING:

a. Ellipsis (the intentional omission of words) in a quoted passage. Retain necessary punctuation preceding the ellipsis:

I do not regret . . . that Canadians pay insufficient heed to their past. . . . It's in the future we shall find our greatness."
—Pierre Trudeau, speech in House of Commons.

The first of the four final periods signals the end of your sentence.

b. Pause, hesitation, emotional stress, etc., in dialogue and interrupted narrative. Do not overuse this:

"Perhaps I'm not fitted to be a mother? Perhaps . . . and if so . . . and how . . . ?"—Doris Lessing, "A Man and Two Women"

5. AFTER A NONSENTENCE. (A nonsentence is a legitimate unit of expression lacking subject + predicate. It is found mostly in dialogue.)

a. A greeting: Good morning.

b. A mild exclamation not within a sentence: Oh.   Shucks.

c. An answer to a question:

When can I get there? *By nine.*

NOTE: A nonsentence is a correct expression. A sentence fragment (a similar structure *un*intentionally lacking subject + predicate) is a serious error. Fragments are explained in G-1.5, page 1.

Do *not* use a period after the title of a composition or report unless that title is a complete sentence:

The Abortion Controversy
Abortion Is a Moral Dilemma.

P-3. The Question Mark [?]

Use a Question Mark

1. AFTER A DIRECT QUESTION.

Are you going? Where? At what time?
It's a long trip, isn't it?
You said—did I hear you correctly?—that you're ready.
You met her at the airport? [A question may be in declarative-sentence form; the question mark signals the tone in which it would be spoken.]

For use of the question mark in quotations, see P-8.8, page 17.

2. WITHIN PARENTHESES TO INDICATE DOUBT OR UNCERTAINTY.

Chaucer was born in 1340 (?) and died in 1400.

Do *Not* Use a Question Mark

3. AFTER AN INDIRECT QUESTION.

Sherwood asked whether I would be there.

4. AFTER A POLITE REQUEST IN QUESTION FORM.

Will you kindly send me a copy of the report.

5. WITHIN PARENTHESES TO EXPRESS HUMOR OR IRONY.

WRONG: They are such a charming (?) couple.

P-4. The Exclamation Point [!]

Use an Exclamation Point

1. AFTER AN EMPHATIC WORD, SENTENCE, OR OTHER EXPRESSION.

Wonderful!   I can't believe it!
Holy cow!   What a play!

Do *Not* Use an Exclamation Point

2. AFTER A MILD INTERJECTION OR A SENTENCE THAT SUGGESTS ONLY MILD EXCITEMENT OR EMOTION. The exclamation point is a strong signal, but one that quickly loses its effect if overused. In general, outside of quoted dialogue, reserve the exclamation point for expressions that begin with *how* or *what* (and are not questions). Elsewhere, use the less dramatic comma or period:

How crude of him!   Why, I never knew that.

3. MORE THAN ONCE, OR WITH OTHER PAUSE OR STOP MARKS.

WRONG: Holy cow!!! [One ! is sufficient.]

WRONG: You sold the cow for a handful of beans?! [Use *either* ? or !]

For use of the exclamation point in quotations, see P-8.8, page 17.

P-5. The Semicolon [;]

The semicolon signals a greater break in thought than the comma but a lesser break than the period. It is, however, closer to a period than to a comma in most of its uses and is often interchangeable with the period. The semicolon is most appropriate in fairly formal writing, as the following examples suggest.

Use a Semicolon

1. BETWEEN INDEPENDENT CLAUSES NOT JOINED BY A COORDINATE CONJUNCTION.

Since the mid-1970's Canada's campuses have been relatively quiet; today's students seem interested more in courses than causes.

The semicolon is particularly effective for showing balance or contrast between the two clauses:

People are usually willing to give advice; they are much less inclined to take it.

The lakes abound with fish; the woods abound with game.

2. BETWEEN INDEPENDENT CLAUSES JOINED BY A CONJUNCTIVE ADVERB (*therefore, however, nevertheless, thus, moreover, also, besides, consequently, meanwhile, otherwise, then, also, furthermore, likewise, in fact, still*)

On weekdays we close at eleven; *however*, on weekends we stay open until one.

Take six courses this semester; *otherwise* you may not graduate.

NOTE: The comma after some conjunctive adverbs is optional.

Some conjunctive adverbs may drift into the second clause, but the semicolon remains between the clauses:

On weekdays we close at eleven; on weekends, *however*, we stay open until one.

NOTE: Use a *comma* before *so*, a coordinate conjunction. See P-1.1, page 12.

3. BETWEEN INDEPENDENT CLAUSES JOINED BY A COORDINATE CONJUNCTION, WHEN THERE ARE COMMAS WITHIN THE CLAUSES.

Today people can buy what they need from department stores, supermarkets, and discount stores; but in earlier times, when such conveniences did not exist, people depended on general stores and peddlers. [The semicolon marks the break between the clauses more clearly than a comma would.]

4. BETWEEN ITEMS IN A SERIES, WHEN THERE ARE COMMAS WITHIN THE ITEMS.

At the high school alumni dinner I sat with the school's best-known graduate, Harper Wyckoff; the editor of the school paper; two stars of the school play, a fellow and a girl who later married each other; and Tad Frump, the class clown.

P-6. The Apostrophe [']

Use the Apostrophe

1. TO FORM THE POSSESSIVE CASE OF NOUNS.

A noun is possessive if it can also be expressed as the last word in an *of* phrase: the *captain's* chair = the chair of the captain.

a. Form the possessives of these with apostrophe + s:

1. Almost all singular nouns:
a woman's coat
Mr. Smith's car
Ms. Davis's boat
a bird's nest
a person's legal right
a fox's bushy tail
the class's performance
Lois's dingy old car

2. Irregular plural nouns that do not end in s:
the women's coats
the people's legal rights
the mice's nest

NOTE: Some authorities favor different rules for singular nouns ending in *s*. Whichever system you follow, be consistent.

b. Form the possessives of these with an apostrophe alone:

1. Plural nouns ending in s:
two girls' coats
the Smiths' car
the Davises' boat
the birds' nests
the boys' gymnasium
the foxes' bushy tails
the classes' performance

2. A few singular nouns that would sound awkward with another s:
Ulysses' travels
Sophocles' irony

CAUTION: Do not confuse the ordinary plural of nouns with the possessive:

ORDINARY PLURAL:
I know the Smiths.
POSSESSIVE PLURAL:
The Smiths' cat died.

c. Note these fine points of apostrophe use:

(1) Joint vs. individual possession: If two or more nouns possess something jointly, only the last noun gets an apostrophe:

Burglars ransacked *Marge and Ed's* apartment.

If each noun possesses a separate thing, each noun gets an apostrophe:

Burglars ransacked both *Donna's* and *Kathy's* apartments.

(2) In hyphenated words, add the apostrophe to the last word only:

My *father-in-law's* remarriage has upset my wife.

(3) Though possessive personal and interrogative pronouns do *not* take apostrophes (*yours, hers, whose,* etc.), possessive indefinite pronouns do: *anybody's, someone's, each other's, someone else's, everybody else's,* etc.

(4) Words expressing time or amount usually form their possessive just as other nouns do: a *dollar's* worth, a *moment's* rest, a *week's* pay, two *weeks'* pay.

2. TO SHOW OMISSION OF LETTERS OR NUMERALS.

don't [do not]
class of '84 [1984]

who's [who is]
goin' [going]

3. FOR CLARITY, TO FORM THE PLURAL OF LETTERS, NUMBERS, SYMBOLS, AND WORDS REFERRED TO AS WORDS.

Try not to use so many *and's*.
Last term she earned straight *A's*.
His *3's* and *5's* look too much alike.
Use *+'s* and *−'s* on the test.
Lola's career waned during the *1970's* [or *1970s*].

Do *Not* Use the Apostrophe

4. WITH POSSESSIVE PERSONAL PRONOUNS (*his, hers, its, ours, yours, theirs*) OR WITH *whose*.

Whose play caused the team's loss in *its* final game? It was not *hers* or *yours*; it was *ours*. [See G-6.9c and U for *its/it's*, etc.]

5. TO FORM THE POSSESSIVE OF INANIMATE OBJECTS (unless the phrase using *of* sounds awkward):

POOR: the *house's* roof
POOR: the *painting's* frame

BETTER: the roof *of the house*
BETTER: the frame *of the painting*

But

POOR: the wait *of an hour*

BETTER: an *hour's* wait

6. TO FORM THE PLURAL OF A PROPER NOUN.

Merry Christmas from the *Altermatts*. [not *Altermatt's*]

P-7. Italics (Underlining)

Italic type, or *italics*, is slanted type, as in the first words of this sentence. In your typing or handwriting, indicate italics by underlining: <u>Saturday Night</u>, *Saturday Night*.

Use Italics to Designate

1. TITLES OF SEPARATE PUBLICATIONS.

a. Books: *The Incomparable Atuk* is a comic novel.

b. Magazines and newspapers: Mr. Stanley reads *Maclean*'s and the *Globe and Mail*.

NOTE: The word *the* is not capitalized or italicized in a newspaper or magazine title.

c. Bulletins and pamphlets: *Bee Production*

d. Plays, films, TV and radio programs, and musical productions:

Shakespeare's *Hamlet* [play]
Return of the Jedi [film]
The Beachcombers [television program]
A Chorus Line [musical production]

e. Poems long enough to be published separately: Tennyson's *In Memoriam*

NOTE: Do not underline (or put within quotation marks) the title of a composition or research paper unless the title contains words that would be underlined anyway, such as the title of a novel:
A Birdwatcher's Paradise   Symbolism in Steinbeck's *East of Eden*

2. NAMES OF SHIPS, AIRCRAFT, AND SPACECRAFT.

Schultz sailed on the *Bonaventure*.
The spacecraft *Columbia* landed without incident.

3. TITLES OF PAINTINGS AND SCULPTURES.

The Blue Boy   *The Thinker*   *Mona Lisa*

NOTE: Some publications, especially some magazines and newspapers, use quotation marks or capitals instead of italics in many of the above situations. Though not wrong, such alternative practices are not recommended.

4. FOREIGN WORDS NOT YET ANGLICIZED.

It was a *fait accompli*.

NOTE: Consult your dictionary to find whether a word of foreign origin is considered a part of the English language, to be written without italics. Do not underline the common abbreviations A.M., P.M., A.D., viz., vs., i.e., e.g., etc.

5. WORDS, LETTERS, FIGURES, OR SYMBOLS REFERRED TO AS SUCH.

The *t* in *often* is silent.
Avoid using *&* for *and* in formal writing.
Claude's *4*'s and *7*'s are indistinct.
Hester earned two *A*'s and three *B*'s.

6. EMPHASIS, where you cannot convey it by the order or choice of your words:

"You are *so* right," Fenwick remarked. [Only italics will convey the speaker's oral emphasis.]
I said that she *was* a good player. [The emphasis on *was* stresses that she no longer is.]

NOTE: Overuse of italics for emphasis is counterproductive because the italicized words no longer stand out sufficiently. Avoid such overuse.

P-8. Quotation Marks [" "]

Quotation marks enclose the exact words of a speaker, certain titles, or words used in a special sense. With one small exception, they are always used in *pairs*.

Use Quotation Marks to Enclose

1. A DIRECT QUOTATION (a speaker's exact words). Note that commas set off each quotation:

MacArthur vowed, "I shall return," as he left the islands.

NOTE: Do not use quotation marks with an *indirect* quotation (a paraphrase or summary of a speaker's words):
MacArthur vowed that he would return.

Observe these fine points of quotation-mark use:

a. With an interrupted quotation, use quotation marks only around the quoted words:

"I heard," said Amy, "that you passed."

b. With an *un*interrupted quotation of several sentences, use quotation marks only before the first sentence and after the last:

WRONG: Jenkins said, "Something's wrong." "I know it." "He should have called by now."
RIGHT: Jenkins said, "Something's wrong. I know it. He should have called by now."

c. With a long *un*interrupted quotation of several paragraphs, use either of the following forms: (1) Put quotation marks at the beginning of *each* paragraph but at the end of only the *last* paragraph. (2) Use no quotation marks at all; instead, indent the entire quotation and type it single-spaced.

d. With a short quotation that is not a complete sentence, use no commas:

Barrie describes life as "a long lesson in humility."

e. Use three periods to show the omission of unimportant or irrelevant words from a quotation (ellipsis—see P-2.4, page 14):

"What a heavy burden is a name that has become . . . famous."
—Voltaire

f. To insert your explanatory words into a quotation, use brackets (not parentheses):

"From a distance it [fear] is something; nearby it is nothing."
—LaFontaine

g. When quoting dialogue, start a new paragraph with each change of speaker:

"He's dead," Holmes announced.
"Are you sure?" the young lady asked, her face blanching.

h. Do not use quotation marks around sets of quoted lines of poetry. Indent and single-space them:

Grow old along with me!
The best is yet to be,
The last of life, for which the first was made.
—R. Browning, "Rabbi Ben Ezra"

However, you may run a very short poetic quotation into your text, using quotation marks (with a slash marking each line break):

Tennyson shows us an aged Ulysses, ". . . an idle king,/ By this still hearth, among these barren crags."

2. TITLES OF SHORT WRITTEN WORKS: POEMS, ARTICLES, ESSAYS, SHORT STORIES, CHAPTERS, SONGS.

"The Bull Calf" is a poem in Irving Layton's *A Red Carpet for the Sun*.
Chapter 1 of *The Guns of August* is titled "A Funeral."
I still get misty-eyed when Loretta sings "Danny Boy."

3. DEFINITIONS OF WORDS.

The original meaning of *lady* was "kneader of bread."

4. WORDS USED IN A SPECIAL SENSE OR FOR A SPECIAL PURPOSE.

Organized crime operates by having its ill-gotten funds "laundered" so that they appear legitimate.

NOTE: Occasionally you will see a slang expression or nickname enclosed in quotation marks, indicating that the writer recognizes the expression to be inappropriately informal. Avoid this apologetic use of quotation marks.

Use Single Quotation Marks [' '] to Enclose

5. A QUOTATION WITHIN A QUOTATION. Think of this construction as a box within a box. Ordinary double quotation marks [" "] provide the wrapping around the outer

box; single quotation marks [' '] provide the wrapping around the inner box. Be sure to place end punctuation within the right box:

> She asked, "Who said, 'Let them eat cake'?"

Use Other Marks with Quotation Marks as Follows:

6. PERIODS AND COMMAS. Always put these marks *inside* closing quotation marks:

> "I see it," whispered Watson. "It's the speckled band."

7. COLONS AND SEMICOLONS. Always put these marks *outside* closing quotation marks:

> Coe barked, "I have nothing to say"; then he left.
> Three students selected "Endymion": Burke, Rizzo, and Stecz.

8. QUESTION MARKS, EXCLAMATION POINTS, AND DASHES. Place these marks *inside* the quotation marks when they belong to the quotation, *outside* otherwise:

> Shauna asked, "Who is my opponent?" [The quotation is the question.]
> Did Shauna say, "I fear no opponent"? [The part outside the quotation is the question.]
> Did Shauna say, "Who is my opponent?" [Both the quotation and the outside part are questions. Use only one question mark—the first one.]
> "I don't believe it!" she exclaimed.
> How furious he was when she muttered, "I don't know"!
> "How could you do—" Cressida began, but faltered.

Do *Not* Use Quotation Marks

9. TO ENCLOSE THE TITLE OF A COMPOSITION OR RE-SEARCH PAPER (unless the title is a quotation):

> WRONG: "Overproduction as a Cause of the Depression"
> RIGHT: Overproduction as a Cause of the Depression

10. TO SHOW THAT A WORD IS INTENDED IRONICALLY OR HUMOROUSLY. Your irony or humor will be more effective if not so blatantly pointed out:

> WRONG: The way she "keeps house" is not to be believed.
> RIGHT: The way she keeps house is not to be believed.

P-9. The Colon [:]

Use the Colon

1. TO INTRODUCE

a. A list (but only after *as follows*, *the following*, or a noun with which the list is in apposition):

> To the mixture, add *the following*: thyme, basil, parsley, and cloves.
> Our backfield consists of four rookies: Tucker, Galgano, Smyth, and Mack. [The four names are appositives of *rookies*]
> We hired Ms. Roe for one reason: her experience. [*Experience* is an appositive of *reason*.]

Do *not* use a colon (or any other punctuation) before a list that fails to meet the above conditions:

> To the mixture, add thyme, basil, parsley, and cloves.
> Our backfield consists of Tucker, Galgano, Smyth, and Mack.
> We hired Ms. Roe for her experience.

b. A long quotation (one or more paragraphs):

> In *The Art of the Novel* Henry James wrote:

The house of fiction has in short not one window, but a million—a number of possible windows not to be reckoned, rather; . . . [quotation continues for one or more paragraphs]

c. A formal quotation or question:

> The Prime Minister declared: "Everyone is against me but the people."
> The question is: what can we do? [or *The question is: What can we do?*]

d. A second independent clause that explains the first clause:

> Potter's motive is clear: he wants the inheritance.

e. The body of a business letter (after the greeting):

> Dear Sir: Dear Ms. Weiner:

NOTE: Use a comma after the greeting of a personal (friendly) letter.

f. The details following an announcement:

> For sale: mountain cabin

g. A formal resolution, after the word *resolved*:

> Resolved: That this council petition the mayor to . . .

h. The words of a speaker in a play (after the speaker's name):

> MACBETH: She should have died hereafter.

2. TO SEPARATE

a. Parts of a title, reference, or numeral:

> TITLE: *Principles of Mathematics*: *An Introduction*
> REFERENCE: Luke 3: 4–13
> NUMERAL: 8:15 P.M.

b. The place of publication from the publisher, and the volume number from the pages, in bibliographies.

> Miller, Jonathan. *The Body in Question*. New York: Random, 1978.
> Jarchow, Elaine. "In Search of Consistency in Composition Scoring." *English Record* 23.4 (1982): 18–19.

P-10. The Dash [—]

The dash is a dramatic mark, signaling an abrupt break in the flow of a sentence. Do not use it for an ordinary pause or stop, in place of a comma, period, or semicolon. On a typewriter, make a dash using two strokes of the hyphen key, with no spaces before, between, or after.

Use the Dash

1. TO SHOW A SUDDEN BREAK IN THOUGHT.

> I'll give—let's see, what can I give?
> Well, if that's how you feel—
> Reardon began, "May I ask—"

2. TO SET OFF A PARENTHETICAL ELEMENT that is long, that sharply interrupts the sentence, or that otherwise would be hard to distinguish:

> The train arrived—can you believe it?—right on time.
> We traveled by foot, in horse-drawn wagons, and occasionally—if we had some spare cash, if the farmers felt sorry for us, or if we could render some service in exchange—atop a motorized tractor.

3. TO EMPHASIZE AN APPOSITIVE.

> He had only one interest—food. [or . . . *interest: food.*]
> Drill, inspections, calisthenics—all are part of army life.
> The basic skills—reading, writing, and mathematics—are stressed here.

NOTE: The colon also emphasizes but imparts a more formal tone than the dash.

4. TO PRECEDE THE AUTHOR'S NAME AFTER A DIRECT QUOTATION.

> "Short words are best and the old words when short are best of all."
>
> —Winston Churchill

P-11. Parentheses [( )]

Use Parentheses (Always in Pairs)

1. TO SET OFF INCIDENTAL INFORMATION OR COMMENT.

Warren Almond (LIB., Montreal-NDG) chairs the committee.

The painting (probably the most original in the exhibition) at first occasioned little notice.

NOTE: Do not overuse parentheses. Use commas to set off ordinary parenthetical (interrupting) expressions. Do not use an opening capital letter or closing period with a sentence in parentheses within a larger sentence.

2. TO ENCLOSE

a. Letters or figures in enumeration:

She is authorized to (1) sign checks, (2) pay bills, and (3) make purchases.

b. References and directions:

The map (see page 70) will help you.

c. A question mark indicating uncertainty:

He was born in 1897(?) in Brandon, Manitoba.

3. FOR ACCURACY, IN LEGAL DOCUMENTS AND BUSINESS LETTERS.

I enclose fifty dollars ($50).

4. WITH OTHER PUNCTUATION MARKS AS FOLLOWS:

a. The comma, semicolon, and period follow the closing parenthesis when the parentheses set off material in a sentence:

If we go (we are still not sure), you may go too.
He deceived us (weren't we foolish?); he was clever.
I believed her (though I can't imagine why).

b. The question mark and the exclamation point go inside the parentheses if the mark belongs to the parenthetical element; otherwise, they go outside.

One of the translators was Aquila (died A.D. 138?).
Have you read the translation of Tyndale (died 1536)?
Snerd asked my fiancée for a date (what gall!).

Do *Not* Use Parentheses

5. TO INDICATE DELETIONS. Instead draw a line through the deleted words.

WRONG: (Never) Seldom have I seen such gall.
RIGHT: ~~Never~~ Seldom have I seen such gall.

6. TO ENCLOSE EDITORIAL COMMENT. Use brackets for this purpose, as explained in the next section.

P-12. Brackets [[ ]]

Use Brackets

1. TO ENCLOSE YOUR EDITORIAL OR EXPLANATORY REMARKS WITHIN A DIRECT QUOTATION.

"At that time, he [Garneau] was not yet an astronaut."

2. WITH *sic* TO MARK THE ORIGINAL WRITER'S ERROR IN MATERIAL YOU ARE QUOTING.

The note ended, "Respectively [sic] yours, Martha."

NOTE: Sic is Latin for "Thus it is." Its use clarifies that the error was made not by you but by the person you are quoting.

3. TO ENCLOSE STAGE DIRECTIONS.

MIRANDA [*sipping her coffee*]: Are you glad to see me?

P-13. The Hyphen [-]

Use the Hyphen

1. TO JOIN CERTAIN COMPOUND WORDS (consult a dictionary to ascertain which):

mother-in-law　　　　　　　　go-getter

2. TO JOIN WORDS USED AS A SINGLE ADJECTIVE BEFORE A NOUN.

Route 303 is a *well-paved* road.
She tried *door-to-door* selling.

NOTE: Do not hyphenate such a modifier when it *follows* a noun as a subject complement: Route 303 is *well paved*. Do not hyphenate such a modifier when the first word is an *-ly* adverb: *freshly baked bread*.

3. WHEN WRITING OUT TWO-WORD NUMBERS FROM 21 TO 99 AND TWO-WORD FRACTIONS.

twenty-two　　　　　　　　three-fourths
fifty-first　　　　　　　　　five twenty-fourths
two hundred ten　　　　　　two hundred twenty-two

Also hyphenate a compound adjective containing a number:

ten-year-old boy　　forty-hour week　　hundred-yard dash
ten-dollar bill　　two- and three-room apartments

4. TO AVOID AMBIGUITY.

AMBIGUOUS: The advertisement was intended for *old train buffs*.
CLEAR: The advertisement was intended for *old-train buffs*.

5. WITH THE PREFIXES *ex-* (WHEN IT MEANS "FORMER"), *self-*, *all-*, AND THE SUFFIX *-elect*.

ex-president　　　　　　　self-confidence
all-conference　　　　　　Premier-elect Doe

NOTE: The modern tendency is to join nearly all prefixes and suffixes to root words without hyphens, except where ambiguity (*recover, re-cover*), or awkwardness (*antiincorporation*) might result or where the root is capitalized (*anti-American, Europe-wide*). Thus *antiterrorist, noninterventionist, semiliterate* (but *semi-independent*, to avoid a double i), *bimonthly, triweekly, citywide*.

6. TO INDICATE WORDS THAT ARE SPELLED OUT AND HESITATION OR STUTTERING. ·

"She wants a d-o-l-l," her mother said.
"I'm f-f-frightened," he stammered.

7. TO DIVIDE A WORD THAT WILL NOT FIT AT THE END OF THE LINE.

The classroom can accom-
modate thirty students.

NOTE: Always put the hyphen at the end of the first line, not at the beginning of the second line. Do not guess where a word should divide; consult your dictionary. See M-3, page 20, for more details on syllabication.

Mechanics

The term *mechanics* is usually understood to include spelling and punctuation, but each of these is important and complex enough to warrant its own section in this book. This section treats the remaining points of mechanics—the technical conventions that apply only to the written form of our language. Correct mechanics in your paper signals that you are a careful writer, taking pains to make your reader's task easier.

M-1. Manuscript Form

1. HANDWRITTEN PAPERS. Use lined white paper 8½ by 11 inches. Write on one side of the paper only, unless your instructor permits otherwise. Do not use paper torn from notebooks. Write on alternate lines unless lines are at least three-eighths of an inch apart. Use black or blue ink. Write legibly; a word difficult to decipher may be marked as an error. Make capital letters clearly distinguishable from low-ercase letters.

2. TYPED PAPERS. Use unlined white bond paper of good quality, 8½ by 11 inches. Type on one side of the paper only. Do not use colored paper or paper that lets type show through. Use a black ribbon; change it before it gets pale. Keep the keys clean.

Use double spacing. Follow standard conventions in typing. If your typewriter does not have a figure *1*, use the lowercase *l*, not capital *I*. Check your paper for typing mistakes; they may be counted as errors if uncorrected.

3. PAPERS DONE ON WORD PROCESSORS. If you are composing your paper by computer word processing, be sure that the system's printing and paper quality, text width, etc., are acceptable. Some publishers and instructors find the quality of dot-matrix printers unsatisfactory.

4. SPACING. Leave margins of 1 inch for the top and sides of each page, and either 1 or 1½ inches at the bottom.

Indent 1 inch for paragraphs in handwritten papers; indent five spaces in typewritten papers. Do *not* indent the first line of a page unless it begins a new paragraph. Do not crowd lines at the bottom of a page; use another sheet even though it will contain only a line or two.

Separate from the text any prose quotations longer than *four lines* or verse quotations of *two or more lines*; use no quotation marks, use single spacing, and indent ten spaces from the left (½ inch in a handwritten paper). Keep shorter prose quotations in the body of the text and enclose them in quotation marks.

5. TITLE. Center the title on the first line of page 1. Leave the next line blank, and begin writing on the third line. See P-2.5, page 14; P-8.9, page 17; and M-2.6, page 19, for punctuation and capitalization of titles. Do not repeat the title after page 1.

6. PAGE NUMBERS. Number all pages, after the first, with Arabic numerals (*2, 3, 4*, etc.) in the upper right-hand corner. Use no periods or parentheses with the numbers.

7. PROOFREADING. Before handing in a paper, read it thoroughly for errors in spelling, punctuation, wording, and sentence construction. If you have many errors, you should rewrite the page or even the whole paper. Otherwise, make changes as follows:

a. Deletions: Draw a horizontal line through words to be deleted. (Do not use parentheses.)

b. Insertions: Write words to be inserted above the line and use a caret (∧) to show point of insertion.

c. Paragraphing: Use the ¶ sign to show the point at which you wish to indicate a new paragraph. Write *No* ¶ if you wish to remove a paragraph indention.

M-2. Capitalization

Use Capital Letters for

1. THE FIRST WORD OF EVERY SENTENCE. This includes quoted sentences:

She said, "The work is finished."

Do *not* capitalize the first word of

a. An indirect quotation (paraphrase): She said *that the work was finished*.

b. A fragmentary quotation: She said that the work was "almost finished."

c. A sentence in parentheses within another sentence: She said (did I tell you?) that the work was finished.

---

2. THE FIRST WORD OF A LINE OF POETRY (unless the poet has used lowercase).

Had we but world enough, and time,
This coyness, lady, were no crime.

—Andrew Marvell, "To His Coy Mistress"

3. WORDS AND PHRASES USED AS SENTENCES.

Why?   Certainly.   Yes, indeed.   Of course.

4. THE FIRST WORD OF A FORMAL QUESTION OR STATEMENT FOLLOWING A COLON.

He asked several questions: Where are you going? What will you do? Where is your goal?
I offer a word of advice: Read only the best books.

5. THE FIRST WORD OF EACH ITEM IN A FORMAL OUTLINE.

I. Sports taught this semester
  A. Swimming
  B. Softball

6. THE FIRST AND LAST WORD AND ALL OTHER IMPORTANT WORDS IN A TITLE.

The Edible Woman [book]
"Champion of the World" [chapter]

Do *not* capitalize

a. Unimportant words in titles: articles (*a, an, the*), coordinate conjunctions (*and, but*, etc.) and prepositions (*to, with, about*, etc.).

b. *The* in titles of newspapers and magazines:

I read the *Globe and Mail*.

But do capitalize *the* when it is the first word in a book title: *The Immigrants*.

---

7. THE FIRST AND LAST WORD IN THE SALUTATION (GREETING) OF A LETTER AND THE FIRST WORD IN THE COMPLIMENTARY CLOSE.

My dearest Son,   Very truly yours,

8. PROPER NOUNS AND ADJECTIVES MADE FROM THEM. A proper noun, as distinguished from a common noun, is the name of a specific person, place, or thing. A proper adjective is made from a proper noun: America, American; Shakespeare, Shakespearean:

Proper Noun	Common Noun
Stella	woman
Thunder Bay	city
July	month
Vanier College	college
Chamber of Commerce	organization

a. Specific persons, races, tribes, nationalities, and languages:

Robertson Davies   Eskimo   English
Italian   Japanese   Latin

NOTE: It is not customary to capitalize *black*, *white*, *aborigine*, and similar racial descriptions.

b. Specific places (countries, states, cities, geographic sections; oceans, lakes, rivers; streets, buildings, rooms, parks, monuments, etc.):

Japan	Atlantic Ocean	Maple Street
Quebec	Lake Algonquin	the Todd Building
Kingston	Mackenzie River	Room 164
the Far East	Fairmount Park	Cenotaph

c. Specific organizations:

the Giants   United Nations   Red Cross
Knights of Colum-   Ace Tire Company
  bus

d. Days of the week, months, and holidays:

Friday   August   Canada Day   Labor Day

e. Religious names considered sacred:

God   Heavenly Father   Yahweh
the Virgin   the Christ Child   Allah
the Lord   the Most High   the Savior

f. Historical events, periods, and documents:

Battle of the Bulge   the Civil Rights Act
the Renaissance   Magna Charta

g. Names of educational institutions, departments, courses, classes of students, and specific academic degrees:

Washboard College   Biology 101 [but see 13
Junior Class   below]
Sc.D. (Doctor of Science)   Department of Philosophy

h. Names of flags, emblems, and school colors:

the Maple Leaf   the Victoria Cross   the Blue and Gold

i. Stars and planets:

the North Star   Mars   the Big Dipper

NOTE: Do not capitalize *sun* and *moon* unless they are personified (considered as persons). Do not capitalize *earth* unless it is personified or considered as one of the planets.

j. Ships, trains, aircraft, and spacecraft:

Titanic   Arrow   Columbia

k. Initials indicating time, divisions of the government, telephone exchanges, call letters of radio and TV stations, and certain other well-known sets of initials:

B.C.	TV	PE 6-5000
RCMP	CN	O.K. (or OK)
CBMT	A.M.	CHMC

l. Personifications:

Mother Nature   Old Man Winter   the eye of Death

m. A title preceding a name:

Professor Jane Melton   Justice Berger
General Burns   the Reverend Beliveau

Do not capitalize a title following a name unless the title shows very high national or international distinction:

Jane Melton, professor of history
Brian Mulroney, Prime Minister of Canada

You may capitalize a title of very high distinction when used instead of the person's name. Be consistent in this usage:

The Prime Minister rose in the House.

Capitalize an abbreviated title before or after a name:

Prof. Susan Zulli, Ph.D.   Sen. Robert Clark, Jr.

9. THE PRONOUN *I* AND THE INTERJECTION O:

May I always worship thee, O Zeus.

NOTE: Do not capitalize *oh* unless some other rule applies.

Do Not Capitalize

10. POINTS OF THE COMPASS (unless they refer to a specific geographic locality):

She flew east from Victoria, not north.
Her family lived in the Middle West.
The Soviets and the West are again in confrontation.

11. SEASONS (unless personified):

Paul goes south every winter.
"Gentle Spring! in sunshine clad . . ."

—Charles D'Orleans, "Spring"

12. WORDS DENOTING A FAMILY RELATIONSHIP, when they follow a possessive noun or pronoun:

I wrote to my mother.   She is Charlie's aunt.

But do capitalize when the family relationship is used as a title preceding a name or by itself as if a name:

Here comes Uncle Sid.   I love you, Father.

13. NAMES OF ACADEMIC DISCIPLINES (unless they are part of specific course titles or proper nouns):

I could never pass mathematics or physics.
I passed Differential Calculus II. [specific course title]
I majored in English and French. [proper nouns]

14. COMMON NOUNS (unless they are part of proper nouns):

I was a senior at the high school in our township.
At Hamilton High School in Tucker Township, I was president of the Senior Class.

15. THE FIRST WORD AFTER A SEMICOLON.

Fay handed in her paper; then she left.

16. THE FIRST WORD IN THE LATTER PART OF AN INTERRUPTED QUOTATION (unless that word begins a new sentence):

"My goal," said Jo, "is to sky-dive." [one quoted sentence]
"I have one goal," said Jo. "It is to sky-dive." [*It* begins a new quoted sentence.]

17. THE FIRST WORD OF A QUOTATION THAT IS NOT A COMPLETE SENTENCE.

She described him as a "bright and serious student."

18. THE SECOND PART OF A COMPOUND WORD (unless it is a proper noun):

Forty-second Street   all-Canadian   ex-Prime Minister
    Trudeau

19. A WORD YOU WANT TO EMPHASIZE (use italics instead):

WRONG: The label said NOT to shake.
RIGHT: The label said *not* to shake.

M-3. Syllabication

Sometimes you must break a word at the end of a line. Avoid doing so whenever possible; especially avoid breaking two successive lines. When breaking a word is unavoidable, mark the division with a hyphen (made with one stroke on the typewriter

[-]). A good dictionary is your most reliable guide to the hyphenation of words. Remembering the following general rules, however, will reduce your need to consult the dictionary.

1. DIVIDE ACCORDING TO PRONUNCIATION; ALWAYS DIVIDE BETWEEN SYLLABLES. Leave enough of a word at the end of the first line to suggest the sound and meaning of the whole word: *com-plete, monot-onous, change-able.*

2. DIVIDE COMPOUND WORDS BETWEEN THE PARTS: *hand-book, book-keeper, rattle-snake.*
If a compound word is already hyphenated, break it at an existing hyphen: *sister-in-law, self-portrait.*

3. DO NOT DIVIDE A ONE-SYLLABLE WORD OF ANY LENGTH: *straight, through, dropped, slipped, found.*

4. DO NOT SET OFF A SINGLE LETTER AS A SYLLABLE:

WRONG: a-way　scar-y　　　　RIGHT: away　scary

M-4. Numbers

1. GENERALLY, WRITE OUT A NUMBER IN WORDS WHEN

a. It will take only one or two words: *forty* bushels, *thirty-nine* steps, *two hundred* spectators, *thirty-third* floor.

b. The number is part of a compound adjective: an *eight-hour* day, a *five-year-old* girl, a *six-room* house.

c. The number is a fraction unaccompanied by a whole number: *one-fourth* of your pay, *two-fifths* of a mile.

NOTE: Use figures otherwise: The house is 4½ miles from Rome.

d. The number begins a sentence:

Three hundred fifty copies were all that the book sold.

Never begin a sentence with a figure. If the number is a long one, rewrite the sentence to place the number elsewhere:

The book sold only *2,876* copies.

2. USE FIGURES FOR

a. Any number that would be three or more words when written out:

This residence houses *138* students.

Use commas to separate every set of three digits (except in serial and telephone numbers, addresses, years in dates, and page numbers). Count from the right or the decimal point:

2,876 copies	*$1,345,009.59*
1066 A.D.	*1456* East Drive

Write very large round numbers as follows:

two million　*23 million*　*4.2 trillion*

b. Dates; addresses; room numbers; telephone numbers; chapter, page, and line numbers; serial numbers; decimals and percentages; route numbers; times; statistics; and precise measurements:

March *20, 1931*	*117* Bly Road	Room *114*
224-8575	Chapter *4*	*998-47-3373*
32.7	*7* percent	Route *6*
3:30 P.M.	*92* for; *37* against	*6* by *3.2* inches [but *six feet long*]

NOTE: Observe these cautions:

(1) Do not use *-st, -th*, etc., after figures in dates:

WRONG: March *15th, 1983*
RIGHT: March *15, 1983* [but *the fifteenth of March*]

(2) In formal writing, do not use the form 3/20/85 for a date.

(3) In writing a time, use figures with A.M. and P.M. and when emphasizing an exact time. Generally, use words otherwise:

3 P.M.	from *2:30* to *3:00* A.M.	at *9:45* tomorrow
four o'clock	around *half-past five*	

c. Groups of numbers in the same passage (do not mix words and figures):

Vote totals by precinct were *135, 78, 10, 166*, and *23*.

3. WRITE AMOUNTS OF MONEY AS FOLLOWS:

I earn *sixty-five dollars* a week. I earn *$65.50* a week.
I earn *$310* a week. I won *$40, $30*, and *$5* at the races.
She won *a million dollars*. She won *$6 million*.
She won *$6,889,346*.

M-5. Abbreviations

Abbreviations are intended mainly for limited spaces, such as signs, telephone directories, and footnotes. In ordinary writing, avoid abbreviations except for those considered acceptable.

Abbreviate

1. CERTAIN TITLES BEFORE PROPER NAMES: *Mr., Mrs., Ms., Dr., St.* (*saint*, not *street*), *Messrs., Mmes.*

Write *Reverend* and *Honorable* in full if they follow *the*:

the *Reverend* Irwin Smyth	the *Honorable* Beatrice Bloom
Rev. Irwin Smyth	*Hon.* Beatrice Bloom

Write military and political titles in full if you use only the person's last name:

Major General Puffington	*Senator* Claghorn
Maj. Gen. John Puffington	*Sen.* Brutus Claghorn

2. CERTAIN TITLES, INCLUDING DEGREES, AFTER PROPER NAMES: *Sr.* (*senior*), *Jr., Esq., M.A., Ph.D.*

Eula B. Smith, *Ed.D.*, is the main speaker.

3. CERTAIN EXPRESSIONS USED WITH NUMERALS: *A.M, P.M., A.D., B.C., No.* (*number*), $:

9:30 A.M　　A.D 1066　　450 B.C　　No. 484　　$43.50

WRONG: She arrived this A.M.
RIGHT: She arrived this *morning*.

4. CERTAIN LATIN PHRASES: *i.e.* (*that is*), *viz.* (*namely*), *e.g.* (*for example*), *cf.* (*compare*), *etc.* (*and so forth*), *vs.* (*versus*).

NOTE: Publishers tend to discourage the use of these abbreviations in the text of formal writing; you would do better to write out the English equivalents unless space is restricted (as in notes).

NOTE: Never write *and etc.*; it is redundant. Avoid *etc.* itself as far as possible; many authorities consider it a lazy writer's crutch.

5. CERTAIN GOVERNMENTAL AGENCIES AND OTHER WELL-KNOWN ORGANIZATIONS: *RCMP, CHMC, CBC, CN.* To be sure your reader knows the meaning of such initials, give the full title the first time:

Leaders of the *Central Intelligence Agency* met with the President. The *CIA* officials had no comment afterward.

Do *Not* Abbreviate

6. NAMES OF PROVINCES, COUNTRIES, MONTHS, DAYS.

WRONG: He left for *B.C.* last *Fri.*
RIGHT: He left for *British Columbia* last *Friday.*

7. PERSONAL NAMES.

WRONG: Is *Geo.* coming home?
RIGHT: Is *George* coming home?

8. THE WORD *Christmas.* (Avoid *Xmas.*)

9. THE WORDS *street, avenue, road, park,* AND *company,* especially as part of a proper name:

WRONG: The Harding *Co.* is on Fifth *St.*
RIGHT: The Harding *Company* is on Fifth *Street.*

10. THE WORD *and*, except in names of firms: *Ways and Means Committee; Smith & Barnes, Inc.*

11. REFERENCES TO A SCHOOL SUBJECT.

WRONG: The *phys. ed.* class was dismissed.
RIGHT: The *physical education* class was dismissed.

12. THE WORDS *volume, chapter,* AND *page* (except in footnotes, tabulations, and technical writing; see a good dictionary for other abbreviations used in such writing).

Effective Paragraphs

A paragraph is a unit of written English. It may consist of only one sentence (as sometimes in dialogue or transition), but more often in general writing it will consist of two or more sentences that are clearly related in meaning. A paragraph is both a *visual entity*—a block of writing with its first line indented and the remainder of its last line left blank—and a *unit of meaning*, a stage in the writer's thought.

Paragraphs vary so greatly in length and structure that it is not possible to give simple paragraphing rules. The following guides, however, reflect the general practice of experienced writers.

¶-1. Organization

1. ESTABLISH A CENTRAL IDEA. Develop your paragraph around a single main idea, usually contained in your **topic sentence**. In most paragraphs the topic sentence appears at the beginning, but it may appear elsewhere—particularly at the end—or only be implied.

a. Topic sentence first:

To me an Indian bazaar is a source of endless delight and excitement. It is usually a series of plain wooden stalls on which are piled, with unconscious artistry, brightly colored fruits, vegetables, spices, gleaming silver jewelry, brilliant silks and cottons, or charming, grotesque painted wooden toys. The vendors who can't afford a stall sit on the sidewalk outside the market, their baskets staked behind them, their wives in vivid cotton saris crouching in the shade, and in front of them are spread carpets of scarlet chillies drying in the sun, small hills of saffron, turmeric, coriander, ginger, cinnamon—all the magical names from the old days of the spice trade with the Indies. With a worn stone mortar and pestle the vendor or his wife will grind your spices for you, blending them according to your particular taste, and weigh them in tiny brass scales strung on twine and balanced delicately in one hand. In all transactions you receive a pleasantly individual attention—nothing is standardized.

—Santha Rama Rau, "Return to India"

b. Topic sentence last:

As the heads of their [the Germans'] columns neared Mons on the 22nd, part of a cavalry squadron scouting the road north of the canal saw a group of four horsemen riding toward them. They looked unfamiliar. At the same instant the strange riders saw the British, and halted. There was a kind of breathless pause before each realized he was looking at the enemy. The Uhlans turned to rejoin the rest of their squadron and galloped back, chased by the British, who caught up with them in the streets of Soignies. In a sharp skirmish the Uhlans were "hampered by their long lances and a good many threw them away." The British killed three or four and left the somewhat restricted field victorious. Captain Hornby, leader of the squadron, was awarded the DSO as the first British officer to kill a German with the new pattern cavalry sword. *The war had opened in correct style with the most encouraging results.*

—Barbara W. Tuchman, *The Guns of August*

c. Topic sentence implied:

Riderless cavalry horses, at many a battle, have been seen to come together and go through their customary evolutions at the sound of the bugle call. Most domestic beasts seem machines pure and simple, undoubtingly, unhesitatingly doing from minute to minute the duties they have been taught, and giving no sign that the possibility of an alternative ever suggests itself to their mind. Men grown old in prison have asked to be re-admitted after being once set free. In a railroad accident a menagerie tiger, whose cage had been broken open, is said to have emerged, but presently crept back again, as if too much bewildered by his new responsibilities, so that he was without difficulty secured.

—William James, *Psychology*

[Implied topic sentence: *Both animals and human beings tend to repeat a deeply ingrained pattern of action, even when presented with a more advantageous alternative.*]

2. DEVELOP THE TOPIC SENTENCE. All the other sentences in your paragraph should support the general idea you stated in your topic sentence. You give such support usually through **facts and examples**, **reasons**, **definition** of a key term, or a **comparison** or **contrast** of two sets of facts or two points of view.

a. Facts and examples:

It is their young who most trouble the Japanese. They are a remarkably law-abiding people. Yet at graduation time this spring, more than 10% of the nation's junior high schools were guarded by the police. A group of teen-agers in Yokohama not long ago beat several street bums to death. Gangs of motorcycle riders taunt the police on Saturday nights; they blast past the stations and dare police to chase them through the maze of traffic. Juvenile delinquency, historically always low, has increased 80% since 1972. A White Paper issued by the Prime Minister's office concluded of today's youth: "They are devoid of perseverance, dependent upon others and self-centered."

—Lance Morrow, "Japan: All the Hazards and Threats of Success"

b. Reasons:

People who talk about "correct English" are usually oversimplifying the problem dangerously. There is no single, monolithic "correct English." There is nothing inherent or intrinsic that makes language "correct." For instance, in America it is considered low-class or "backwoodsy" to say "He et his dinner." In England, however, *et*, as the past tense of *eat*, has the highest prestige, and the best-spoken Englishmen will say "He et his dinner." It is simply a matter of differing usage, in one social group or another. Even good speakers have several styles at their command—not only the formal English of the purists, but an easy, informal English for conversational situations. Good English is that which is appropriate and effective, even when it goes against the pronouncements of purists.

—Allan Walker Reed, "Is American English Deteriorating?"

c. Definition:

What you need, of course, is a reasonable definition of science fiction, one that distinguishes it from the non-SF sometimes mistakenly shelved with it. The best place to begin defining is with the name, *science fiction*. The second word first. *Fiction* signals a kind of literature. In form, then, SF should have the basic fictional ingredients of a story—plot, character, setting, action, point of view. In function, SF, like all forms of literature, should tell us something about the human experience. Now to the second word, the qualifier, *science*. This crucial word separates SF from other fiction genres like fantasy, westerns, and the occult. What makes SF is the science, real or imaginary; without it there is no science fiction. Putting the two halves together produces a general formula that should subsume most SF material— "most" because no literary definition is totally inclusive or exclusive. *Science fiction is the branch of literature that imaginatively speculates on the consequences of living in a scientific or technological world.*

—Gary Goshgarian, "Zeroing In on Science Fiction"

d. Comparison:

Primitive magic survives in the subconscious. The strand of hair carried in the locket, grandmother's wedding dress, the faded fan of the first ball, the regimental badge, all have a half-conscious fetish character. The bobby-soxers who tear shreds off the crooner's garb are the vulgarized twentieth-century version of the worshipers cherishing a splinter from a saint's bone. The value that we set on original manuscripts, on "signed" pieces of furniture, on Dickens' quill and Kepler's telescope, are more dignified manifestations of the same unconscious tendency. It is, as the child said, "jolly nice" to behold a fragment of a marble by Praxiteles—even if it is battered out of human shape, with a leper's nose and broken ears. The contact with the master's hand has imbued it with a magic quality which has lingered on and radiates at us, conveying the same thrill as "the real blood on Nelson's real shirt."

—Arthur Koestler, *The Anatomy of Snobbery*

e. Contrast:

The motives that brought Spaniards and Englishmen to America also differed. The former came on an enterprise of discovery, searching for a new route to India initially, and later for new lands to conquer, the fountain of youth, minerals, the Seven Cities of Cibola and, in the case of the missionaries, new souls to win for the Kingdom of Heaven. The English came to escape religious persecution, and once having found a haven, they settled down to cultivate the soil and establish their homes. Since the Spaniards were not seeking a refuge or running away from anything, they continued their explorations and circled the globe 25 years after the discovery of the New World.

—Arthur L. Campa, "Anglo vs. Chicano: Why?"

CAUTION: Many inexperienced writers fail to develop paragraphs adequately. They merely repeat several times, in different words, the general statement of their topic sentence or make further, unsupported generalizations based on the topic sentence. Avoid such undeveloped paragraphs by including sufficient specifics (facts, reasons, and so forth) to convince the reader of the validity of your topic sentence.

UNDEVELOPED: Today's college campuses display a fascinating variety of building styles. Some structures are radically different from others in architecture. Very old buildings may stand beside ultramodern edifices. The variety of structures truly fascinates me on my visits to college campuses.

FULLY DEVELOPED: Today's college campuses display a fascinating variety of architecture. Pseudo-Gothic Victorian towers may abut geodesic domes bulging from concrete plazas. At the State University's main campus a sheer twenty-story steel-and-glass tower gleams at one end of the Quadrangle; an ornate but grimy turn-of-the-century stone fortress scowls from behind massed shrubbery at the other. Between the two squat utilitarian postwar cement-block dorms indistinguishable from army barracks. Most older campuses yield similar examples. Such architectural cacophony is, nevertheless, fascinating in its very horror.

¶-2. Unity

If your paragraph is to make a unified impression, each sentence must stand in clear relation to the topic sentence. During revision, try to spot any sentences that lead away from the main idea of the paragraph. Delete them. In the first paragraph below, sentences that weaken unity appear in italics:

NOT UNIFIED: The ancient Greeks and Romans pioneered solar heating more than 2,500 years ago. *The Greeks also invented the flush toilet, central heating, and some other supposedly modern conveniences.* It was a shortage of wood, not oil, that led the Greeks to use the sun as a source of energy. The ancient town of Olynthus in northern Greece consisted entirely of houses designed to gather as much heat from the sun as possible. The north sides of these houses were closed, and the main living areas faced the warmer south side. In ancient Rome the building of a structure that blocked a neighbor's sunlight was illegal. *Many modern communities are considering similar laws today.*

UNIFIED: The ancient Greeks and Romans pioneered solar heating more than 2,500 years ago. It was a shortage of wood, not oil, that led the Greeks to use the sun as a source of energy. The ancient town of Olynthus in northern Greece consisted entirely of houses designed to gather as much heat from the sun as possible. The north sides of these houses were closed, and the main living areas faced the warmer south side.

In ancient Rome the building of a structure that blocked a neighbor's sunlight was illegal.

¶-3. Coherence

Just as your paragraph has unity when no sentence leads away from the idea of the topic sentence, it has coherence when your thought flows smoothly from the first sentence through the last. Two devices that will help you achieve coherence in a paragraph are *transitional expressions* and *repetition of key words or phrases*.

1. **TRANSITIONAL EXPRESSIONS.** Such expressions show the relationship between sentences or parts of sentences. Transitional expressions do the following:

   a. **Indicate stages of thought:** *first, second,* and so forth; *in conclusion, finally, consequently.*

   b. **Signal that more evidence is coming:** *in addition, moreover, next, also, that is.*

   c. **Mark a change in direction:** *however, yet, still, on the other hand, nevertheless.*

   d. **Show relationships:** *even more important, above all, in particular, then, formerly, at the same time, at last, beyond, further.*

   e. **Signal a conclusion:** *therefore, then, thus, in sum, on the whole.* Avoid the trite *in conclusion.*

   To be reliable, testimony must be disinterested. *That is,* it must come from a person who does not stand to gain from his or her statement. If several witnesses swear that they saw the defendant in a robbery case lurking near the bank just before a holdup, the jury is likely to believe them. *On the other hand,* the defense attorney can render their testimony worthless if he or she can show that these witnesses have something to gain by casting suspicion on the defendant. The question of disinterestedness is not a concern of the courtroom only. It must *also* be considered by historians trying to establish the truth about the past, legislators trying to draft fair laws, and ordinary citizens trying to determine the credibility of their leaders.

2. **REPETITION OF KEY WORDS.** Words and phrases that are essential to the subject matter of the paragraph provide signposts to your reader as you repeat them in the paragraph or restate them in easily recognized synonyms. In addition, your use of pronouns that refer clearly to previously mentioned nouns can aid in achieving coherence. Key words in the following paragraph are italicized.

   All *science* is the *search* for unity in hidden *likenesses*. The *search* may be on a grand scale, as in the modern theories which try to link the fields of gravitation and electromagnetism. But we do not need to be browbeaten by the scale of *science*. There are discoveries to be made by snatching a small *likeness* from the air too, if it is bold enough. . . .

—Jacob Bronowski, *Science and Human Values*

¶-4. Paragraph Length

1. **PARAGRAPHING FOR EMPHASIS.** Paragraphing makes the parts of a composition distinct. One or two important sentences may deserve a paragraph of their own; less important details should be worked into a longer paragraph with other material.

2. **DETERMINING THE LENGTH OF A PARAGRAPH.** The lengths of paragraphs naturally vary according to their content. In ¶-1 through ¶-3, the examples of well-written paragraphs range from four sentences (mostly long ones) to ten sentences. Introductory and concluding paragraphs, along with those given special emphasis, are often shorter.

3. **PARAGRAPHING DIALOGUE.** In writing dialogue, start a new paragraph with each change of speaker. It is a good idea to break long speeches by the same speaker into paragraphs. See P-8.1g, page 16, for punctuation of dialogue.

Spelling

Misspelling is the gravy stain of writing. Misspelled words affect your reader the way a large glob of gravy on your best suit or dress would affect someone you were trying to impress. Because misspelling and incompetence are usually associated in a reader's mind, you need to make every effort to purge faulty spelling habits from your writing. Consult a dictionary whenever you doubt the spelling of a word. Keep a list of words you frequently misspell, and try to analyze the reasons for your recurring errors. Except in rare cases, you can correct them by attention to one or more of the following suggestions.

S-1. Techniques for Spelling Improvement

To Improve Your Spelling:

1. **VISUALIZE THE CORRECT SPELLING OF A WORD.** Look attentively at a word; then look away from it and try to see, in your mind, the word before you on a page.

2. **PRACTICE PRONOUNCING AND SPELLING TROUBLESOME WORDS ALOUD, SYLLABLE BY SYLLABLE.**

   ath-let-ic   quan-ti-ty
   en-vi-ron-ment   ac-ci-den-tal-ly
   gov-ern-ment   lab-or-a-to-ry

3. **PRACTICE WRITING A TROUBLESOME WORD SEVERAL TIMES.** Begin slowly and increase your speed until the right form comes easily. You will need drill to substitute correct spelling habits for faulty ones.

4. **DISTINGUISH BETWEEN WORDS SIMILAR IN SOUND OR SPELLING.** See S-2, page 25, and U, pages 27–31, for explanations of the following and many other such distinctions:

   to/too/two   lose/loose   its/it's   whose/who's
   your/you're   there/their/they're   woman/women

5. **DO NOT DROP, ADD, OR CHANGE LETTERS WHEN ADDING PREFIXES OR SUFFIXES OR COMBINING ROOTS,** unless you know that a spelling rule applies (see 6b–6e below):

Prefix + Root	Root + Suffix	Root + Root
dis|appear	careful|ly	book|keeper
dis|satisfied	immediate|ly	grand|daughter
mis|spell	comical|ly	
re|commend	state|ment	
im|moral		

6. **MASTER THESE SPELLING RULES.**

   a. *ie* and *ei*: This version of the old jingle should help you:

   When the sound is like *EE*,
   Put *i* before *e*—
   Except after *c*.

   That is, when the sound of the two letters is *EE* (as in *see*), use *ie* (*chief, grief, niece, hygiene, field, relief*, unless a *c* precedes (*receive, conceit, ceiling, deceive*). When the sound is not *EE*, write *ei* (*eight, height, their, foreign, counterfeit, veil*).

   Remember these odd sentences for the common exceptions:

   ie: The financier's species is friendly.
   ei: Neither weird protein seizes leisure.

   NOTE: The *ie* jingle does not apply when the *i* and *e* are in separate syllables (*sci ence*).

   b. Final e: Drop a final silent *e* before a suffix beginning with a **vowel** or y (*a, e, i, o, u, y*):

   write + ing = writing   fame + ous = famous
   love + able = lovable   scare + y = scary
   hope + ed = hoped   come + ing = coming

   Keep the *e* when the suffix does not begin with a vowel: hope\|ful, love\|less, lone\|ly, safe\|ty, state\|ment, same\|ness.

   Keep the *e* before a vowel suffix

   (1) After *c* or *g*, when the suffix begins with *a* or *o* (to maintain the "soft" *c* or *g* sound): notice\|able, change\|able, courage\|ous.

   (2) To avoid confusion with other words: *singe + ing = singe\|ing* (to avoid confusion with *singing*); *dye + ing = dye\|ing*.

   c. Final y: Change a final *y* to *i* before any suffix except *-ing*:

   happy + ness = happiness   cry + ed = cried
   busy + ly = busily   lady + s = ladies

   cry\|ing   bury\|ing   try\|ing

   Ignore this rule if a vowel precedes the *y*:
   chimney\|s   annoy\|ed   monkey\|s

   EXCEPTIONS: lay, laid; pay, paid; say, said.

   d. Double a final consonant before a suffix beginning with a vowel (including *y*):

   (1) If the consonant ends a one-syllable word and is preceded by a single vowel (*drop, drop\|ping; bat, bat\|ter*) but not if the consonant is preceded by two vowels (*droop, droop\|ing; fail, fail\|ing*).

   (2) If the consonant ends an accented syllable of the root word and is preceded by a single vowel (*oc\|cur, oc-cur\|red; con\|trol, control\|ling*) but not if the last syllable is unaccented (*ben\|efit, benefit\|ed; off\|er, offer\|ing*).

   e. Forming plurals: To form most plurals, add *-s* to the singular (*toy, toys; dollar, dollars;* Don *Remington,* the *Remingtons*). The following generalizations cover most other plurals. Consult your dictionary in other cases or when in doubt.

   (1) Add *-es* to the singular when making a word plural creates an extra syllable: *bush, bush\|es; fox, fox\|es; buzz, buzz\|es; church, church\|es.*

   (2) Add *-es* when the final *y* rule applies (see *c* above): *sky, skies; liberty, liberties.*

   (3) With the following and a few other nouns, change the final *f* or *fe* to *v* and add *-es: calf, calves; knife, knives; wife, wives; loaf, loaves; wharf, wharves; life, lives.*

   (4) With certain singular nouns ending in *o*, add *-es: tomato, tomatoes; potato, potatoes; hero, heroes.* With almost all other singular nouns ending in *o*, add just *-s.* (Musical terms, such as *solo, piano, alto*, and words ending in a vowel + *o*, such as *radio, studio*, always add just *-s.*) With a few final *o* words, you may use either *-s* or *-es: domino, dominos* or *dominoes; zero, zeros* or *zeroes.* Consult a dictionary for plurals of other final *-o* words.

(5) When pluralizing a compound noun, add the -*s* or -*es* to the very end if the compound has no hyphen: *cupfuls, strongboxes.* If the compound is a hyphenated noun plus modifier (*father-in-law*), pluralize the noun: *fathers-in-law, passers-by.*

(6) With certain nouns of foreign origin, use the foreign plural: *alumnus, alumni; alumna, alumnae; stimulus, stimuli; crisis, crises; oasis, oases; hypothesis, hypotheses; parenthesis, parentheses; thesis, theses; analysis, analyses; axis, axes; synopsis, synopses.*

NOTE: With many other such nouns, you may use either the foreign or English plural: *radius, radii* or *radiuses; stadium, stadia* or *stadiums; octopus, octopi* or *octopuses; index, indices* or *indexes; appendix, appendices* or *appendixes; antenna, antennae* (of insects) or *antennas* (of TV sets); *phenomenon, phenomena* or *phenomenons; criterion, criteria* or *criterions; vertebra, vertebrae* or *vertebras.* Many of these use the foreign plural in scholarly or technical writing and the English plural in general writing. Your dictionary may specify when each should be used.

(7) With numbers, letters, and symbols, add '*s* for clarity: *a's, 6's, +'s, and's, 1970's* [or *1970s*].

7. MAKE FULL USE OF MEMORY DEVICES. Associate one word with another, find a word within a word, or make up jingles or nonsense sentences; such **mnemonics** can help you over the trouble spots in your problem words:

Emma is in a *dilemma.*
She put a **dent** in the *superintendent.*

Stationery is pap**er**.
A *principle* is a **rule**.
Poor *grammar* will **mar** your writing.
It is **vile** to have no *privileges*.
The *villain* owns a *villa in* Spain.
There is **a rat** in *separate* and in *comparative*.
I have **lice** on my *license!*
Rage can lead to *tragedy*.
There is **iron** in the *environment*.
There is a **meter** in the *cemetery*.
Tim has great *optimism*.
With any *professor*, one **F** is enough.
An **engine** has plenty of *strength*.

Group words with similar characteristics, such as two sets of double letters (*accommodate, embarrass, possess*) or three *i*'s (*optimistic, primitive*) or names of occupations (*author, censor, conductor, emperor, investor, sponsor, professor*) or the three -*ceed* words (If you *proceed* to *exceed*, you will *succeed*. All other words ending in the same sound are spelled with -*cede*, except *supersede*).

8. PROOFREAD YOUR COMPLETED MANUSCRIPT. Doing so will help you detect—and correct—all misspelled words. Use a dictionary when in doubt.

S-2. Words Similar in Sound

Distinguish between words that are identical or confusingly similar in sound. Many are explained below; those that need more detailed explanation are discussed in Usage (U), pages 27–31.

accept, except. See Usage (U).

advice (noun): counsel: take my *advice*
advise (verb): to give advice: I *advise* you

affect, effect. See U.

all ready, already. See U.

all right: *Alright* is not an accepted spelling.

all together, altogether. See U.

brake (noun): stopping device: apply the *brake*
brake (verb): to cause to stop: *brake* the car
break (verb): to smash: *break* the record

canvas: cloth: a *canvas* tent
canvass: to solicit: *canvass* the area for votes

capital, capitol. See U.

carat: a unit of weight: ten-*carat* diamond
caret: a mark of omission (∧): I ∧ going home
carrot: a vegetable: eat your *carrot*

close (rhymes with *nose*): to shut: *close* the door
clothes: garments: her Sunday *clothes*
cloths (rhymes with *moths*): pieces of cloth: wipe with clean *cloths*

coarse: rough, not fine: *coarse* sandpaper
course: a path; a series of lectures: a race *course*; a college *course*

complement, compliment. See U.

council, counsel, consul. See U.

decent: moral: a *decent* person
descent: a going down; ancestry: a steep *descent*; Irish *descent*
dissent: disagreement: a strong *dissent*

device (noun): an invention, piece of equipment: a clever *device*.
devise (verb): to invent: *devise* a better mousetrap

diary: a journal: write in my *diary*
dairy: a milk farm or store: the *dairy* sells milk

discus: a disc-shaped object: throw the *discus*
discuss: to talk: *discuss* the topic
disgust: to be offensive to: war *disgusts* me

elicit: to draw forth: *elicit* a response
illicit: illegal: *illicit* drugs

eminent: distinguished: an *eminent* educator
imminent: about to happen: rain is *imminent*

envelop (verb): to surround: fog *envelops* us
envelope (noun): container for a letter: seal the *envelope*

formally: according to proper form: *formally* introduced
formerly: previously: *formerly* a sailor

forth: forward: go *forth* and conquer
fourth: 4th: the *fourth* in line

hear: to perceive with the ear: I *hear* you
here: in this place: come *here*

instance, instants, instant's. See U.

irrelevant: extraneous: *irrelevant* to the topic
irrevelant: There is no such word.
irreverent: not reverent: *irreverent* laughter in church

isle: an island: the *Isle* of Wight
aisle: a passage between rows: walk down the *aisle*

its, it's. See U.

later, latter. See U.

lead, led. See U.

lessen: to diminish: *lessen* his ardor
lesson: a unit of instruction: a French *lesson*

loose, lose. See U.
moral, morale. See U.

passed (verb): past tense of *pass*: I *passed* the test
past (noun): a former time: forget the *past*
past (preposition): beyond: walk *past* the house

personal: private: a *personal* question
personnel: members of an organization: notify all *personnel*

piece: a fragment: a *piece* of the puzzle
peace: quietness; absence of war: the Nobel *peace* prize

presence: being present; attendance: demand their *presence*
presents: gifts: birthday *presents*

principal, principle.   See U.

precede: to come before: *1 precedes 2*
proceed: to go forward: the parade *proceeded*

prophecy (noun):   a prediction: an ominous *prophecy*
prophesy (verb):   to predict: she *prophesied* disaster

quiet: not noisy: peace and *quiet*
quite: very, completely: not *quite* ready
quit: stop; give up: *quit* smoking

respectfully, respectively.   See U.

right: correct: the *right* answer
rite: a ceremony: an initiation *rite*
write: to record: *write* this down

sight, cite, site.   See U, under *cite*.

stationary: not moving: *stationary* equipment
stationery: writing paper: letterhead *stationery*

than (conjunction):   compared with: better *than* I
then: at that time: I knew her *then*

their, there, they're.   See U.

threw: past tense of *throw*: he *threw* the ball
through: from end to end of: *through* the tunnel
thorough: complete; exact: a *thorough* search

to, too, two.   See U.

weak: not strong: *weak* from sickness
week: seven days: a *week* from now

weather: rain, shine: stormy *weather*
whether: if: *whether* or not

who's: who is: *who's* there?
whose: possessive of *who*: a man *whose* word is law

woman: one female: a *woman* of renown
women: more than one female: two *women* of renown

your: possessive of *you*: *your* rent is due
you're: you are: *you're* fired

S-3. 170 Words Often Misspelled

Learn to spell correctly the first ten words on the list. When you have mastered the first group of ten, move on to the second group, then the third, and so on. With effort and persistence, you will be able to make a noticeable improvement in your ability to spell these words correctly.

1.
absence
accidentally
accommodate
achievement
acknowledge
acquaintance
acquire
acquitted
across
adolescence

2.
aggressive
amateur
anxious
apologize
apparent
argument
article
athlete
auxiliary
believe

3.
benefited
business
category
cemetery
changeable
character
comparatively
competent
competition
conceivable

4.
condemn
conscientious
conscious
criticism
curiosity
deceive
definite
describe
description
desirable

5.
desperate
develop
disappear
disappoint
disastrous
discipline
dissatisfied
dilemma
diligent
does

6.
ecstasy
eighth
embarrass
entirely
environment
erroneous
etc.
exaggerate
excellent
excitable

7.
exhilaration
existence
familiar
fascinating
fictitious
finally
forcibly
foreign
forfeit
forty

8.
fulfill
government
grammar
guarantee
height
hindrance
hypocrisy
incidentally
independent
indispensable

9.
intelligence
irresistible
kindergarten
knowledge
laboratory
maintenance
maneuver
mathematics
meant
millionaire

10.
mischievous
misspelled
mosquito
necessary
niece
ninety
ninth
noticeable
nucleus
occasionally

11.
occurred
occurrence
omission
omitted
opinion
opportunity
optimistic
outrageous
parallel
pastime

12.
peaceable
perceive
perform
permissible
perseverance
persistent
personally
pertain
possession
preceding

13.
prejudice
prevalent
primitive
privilege
procedure
proceed
professor
psychology
pursue
questionnaire

14.
receive
recommend
religious
reminisce
repetition
restaurant
rhythm
ridiculous
sacrilegious
schedule

15.
seize
sense
sensible
separate
sergeant
shining
similar
sophomore
souvenir
strength

16.
superintendent
supposed to
suppression
surprise
synonym
tendency
tragedy
truly
twelfth
tyranny

17.
unnecessary
unusual
used to
usually
vacuum
vengeance
villain
weird
writing
written

Usage

Certain words and expressions are frequently misused. Others are considered by most authorities to be unsuitable for formal writing and speaking; these include **colloquialisms** (expressions suitable for informal use only), **regionalisms** (those known only in certain areas), and **slang** (those used only among certain social groups and usually short-lived). Still other expressions are considered **nonstandard** or **illiterate** (always to be avoided). Authorities may disagree on the extent to which some words are acceptable. Consider any leading dictionary a reliable guide.

U. Use the Right Word

a, an.   Use *a* before a word beginning with a consonant sound: *a* car, *a* hat, *a* history test, *a* union (*u* pronounced like consonant *y*).
   Use *an* before a word beginning with a vowel sound: *an* accident, *an* image, *an* honest person (*h* is silent), *an* uncle.

about, around, round.   *Around* suggests or specifies encirclement: The children ran *around* the house.
   About and *round* indicate incomplete encirclement: The children clustered *about (round)* the windows.

accept, except.   *Accept* (a verb) means "to receive": She *accepted* the gift.
   Except (usually a preposition) means "excluding": Everyone clapped *except* Farley.

NOTE: Except is occasionally a verb, meaning "to exclude": If you *except* the fifth clause, the rule applies fully in her case.

actual fact, real fact, true fact.   Usually redundant; if a fact is a fact, it is *actual*, *real*, or *true*. Omit such words unless needed to distinguish between an *alleged* or *supposed* fact and an *actual* fact.

adapt, adopt.   *Adapt* means "to adjust or make suitable." It is usually followed by *to*: He *adapted to* his new social environment.
   Adopt means "to take as one's own": He *adopted* the habits of his new social environment. They *adopted* a child.

affect, effect.   Most commonly, *affect* (verb) means "to influence": The war *affected* everyone.
   Most commonly, *effect* (noun) means "a result": One *effect* of the war was mass starvation.

NOTE: Less commonly, *affect* (as a verb) means "to pretend or imitate": He *affected* a British accent. *Effect* (as a verb) means "to accomplish, to bring about": The medicine *effected* a cure.

aggravate.   Colloquial when used for *irritate* or *annoy:* The children *annoyed* (not *aggravated*) him.

ain't.   A nonstandard contraction; avoid it always. Instead use *I'm not, you (we, they) aren't, he (she, it) isn't.*

all, all of.   *All of* is redundant when used with common nouns: *All* (not *all of*) the men arrived on time.

allude, refer.   *Allude* applies to an indirect reference that is not specific: She *alluded* to the Bible.
   Refer identifies specifically: She *referred* to the plague of locusts in Egypt.

allusion, illusion, delusion.   *Allusion* means "an indirect reference." (See *allude*.)
   Illusion means "a false perception eventually recognized as false": It was an optical *illusion*.
   Delusion refers to a false perception or belief that is held as a result of self-deception: She labored under the *delusion* that pink elephants were climbing the wall.

a lot, alot, allot.   *A lot* is colloquial when used for *many* or *much*: He had *many* (not *a lot of*) relatives. He was *much* (not *a lot*) better.
   Alot is a misspelling.
   Allot means "to apportion or give by some plan": The officials will *allot* each large family a subsidy.

already, all ready.   Use *all ready* (meaning "fully ready") wherever *ready* alone makes sense: Dinner was *all ready*. (Dinner was *ready*.)
   Elsewhere, use *already* (meaning "previously" or "by this time"): She had *already* eaten. He is here *already*.

alright.   Incorrect for *all right*.

altogether, all together.   Use *all together* (meaning "in a group") wherever *together* alone makes sense: We were *all together* at the party. (We were *together* at the party.)
   Elsewhere, use *altogether* (meaning "wholly, completely, in all"): The infantry was *altogether* surprised at Dieppe.

alumna, alumnus.   An *alumna* is a female former student of a school or college. The plural is *alumnae* (usually pronounced with a final sound of *EE*).
   An *alumnus* is the male or mixed-gender equivalent; the plural is *alumni* (usually pronounced with a final sound of *EYE*).

amoral, immoral.   *Amoral* means "not concerned with morality": An infant's acts are *amoral*.
   Immoral means "against morality": Murder is *immoral*.

amount, number.   *Amount* refers to things in bulk or mass: a large *amount* of grain. No *amount* of persuasion could change his mind.
   Number refers to countable objects: a *number* of apples.

and etc.   Redundant; *etc.* by itself means "and so forth":
   WRONG: He ordered books, pencils, *and etc.*
   RIGHT: He ordered books, pencils, *etc.*

and/or.   Avoid it except in legal and business writing:
   WEAK: Linda plans to get a degree in psychology *and/or* education.
   BETTER: Linda plans to get a degree in psychology, education, or both.

anyways.   Nonstandard; use *anyway* or *any way*.

angry at, about, with.   One becomes *angry at* or *about* a thing but *angry with* a person. See also *mad*.

anyone, any one.   *Anyone* means "any person": Has *anyone* here seen Kelly?
   Any one refers to any single item of a number of items: If you like my drawings, take *any one* you wish.

anyone, everyone, someone, anybody, everybody, somebody.   Use a singular verb and pronoun with these words. See G-9.5, and G-9.14, page 9.

anyplace, everyplace, noplace, someplace.   Colloquial. Precise writers or speakers prefer *anywhere, everywhere, nowhere, somewhere.*

anywheres, everywheres, nowheres, somewheres.   Nonstandard; use *anywhere, everywhere*, etc.

apt, likely, liable.   *Apt* is used when probability is based on normal, habitual, or customary tendency: She is *apt* to blush when embarrassed.
   Likely indicates mere probability: It is *likely* to rain tomorrow.
   Liable indicates an undesirable or undesired risk: He's *liable* to harm himself by playing with a loaded gun.

aren't I.   Obviously ungrammatical (*are I not*), though some authorities accept it in informal use. *Am I not* is the alternative.

as, because, since.   To express cause, make *because* your first choice; it is most precise.
   As and *since* may be ambiguous, conveying either a time or cause relation: *Since* you left, I've been sick.
   Since is acceptable informally when there is no ambiguity. *As* is the least acceptable.

27

as, like. See *like*.

as for my part. An incorrect combination of *as for me* and *for my part*.

at. Redundant with *where*: *Where* is she? (not *Where* is she *at*?)

aural. See *verbal*.

awful, awfully. *Awful* is colloquial when used to mean "very bad, ugly, shocking": His language was *shocking* (not *awful*).

Awful is incorrect when used adverbially to mean "very": That pizza was *very* (not *awful*) good.

Awfully is colloquial when used to mean "very": Jan is *very* (not *awfully*) happy.

awhile. Do not use the adverb *awhile* after *for*. One may stay *awhile* (adverb), stay a *while* (noun), stay for a *while* (noun), but not for *awhile* (adverb).

bad, badly. *Badly* (adverb) is colloquial when used for *very much* or *greatly* or after a linking verb (*be, seem*, etc.; see G-5.1,2,3, page 5): She wanted *very much* (not *badly*) to be there.

Bad (adjective) correctly follows a linking verb: I feel *bad*.

balance. Correct in *bank balance*. Colloquial when used for the *remainder*, the *rest*: The *rest* (not the *balance*) of the guests left.

because. See *reason is because* and *as, because, since*.

being as (how), being that. Colloquial or nonstandard for *as, because*, or *since* (which see).

beside, besides. *Beside* (preposition) means "by the side of": No one was sitting *beside* me [the seat next to mine was empty].

Besides (preposition) means "in addition to" or "except": No one was sitting *besides* me [everyone else was standing]. As a conjunctive adverb, it means "in addition": He is ugly; *besides*, he is boorish.

better, had better. Always add *had* or its contraction, *'d*, before *better* when you mean *should* or *ought to*:

WRONG: You *better* milk the cows.

RIGHT: You *had* (or You*'d*) better milk the cows.

between, among. *Between* implies *two* persons or things in a relationship; *among* implies *three or more*: Must I decide *between* cake and ice cream? The estate was divided *among* the five children.

born, borne. For all meanings of *bear* except "give birth" the past participle is *borne*. *Borne* is correct in this sense also when it follows *have* or precedes *by*: Mrs. Jackson had already *borne* six children. The half-sisters were *borne* by different mothers.

Born is the correct past participle in other contexts relating to birth: The child was *born* in Brazil. He was *born* into a musical family.

bring, take. Precise usage requires *bring* when you mean "to come (here) with" and *take* when you mean "to go (there) with."

bust, busted, bursted. Incorrect forms of the verb *burst*, of which the three principal parts are *burst, burst, burst*: Yesterday the water pipes *burst* (or *had burst*).

but that, but what. Colloquial for *that*: I don't doubt *that* (not *but that*) he'll come.

buy. Colloquial when used as a noun to mean "purchase": He made a good *purchase* (not a good *buy*).

can, may. *Can* means "to be able": *Can* he lift the log?

May means "to have permission": *May* I go with you?

can't hardly, can't scarcely. A double negative. Say "I *can't* hear her" or "I *can hardly* (or *can scarcely*) hear her."

can't help but. Colloquial for *can't help*:

COLLOQUIAL: I *can't help but* admire him.

FORMAL: I *can't help* admiring him.

FORMAL: I *can but* admire him.

can't seem to. Colloquial for *seem unable to*.

capital, capitol. Use *capitol* only for the building where a legislature meets: The senator posed on the steps of the state *capitol*.

Elsewhere, use *capital*: Toronto is the provincial *capital* [chief city]. The firm has little *capital* [money]. It was a *capital* [first-rate] idea. The defendant has committed a *capital* offense [one punishable by death].

casual, causal. *Casual* means "occurring by chance, informal, unplanned"; *causal* means "involving cause."

cite, site, sight. *Cite* means "quote an authority or give an example": He will *cite* Shakespeare's sonnet about age.

Site means "location": Here is the new building *site*.

Sight refers to vision: His *sight* was as good as it had been when he was twelve years old.

compare to, compare with. *Compare to* means "to point out one or more similarities": Sports writers are *comparing* the rookie *to* Willie Mays.

Compare with means "to examine in order to find similarities and differences": Have you *compared* the new Ford *with* the Plymouth?

complected. Nonstandard for *complexioned*: He was a light-*complexioned* (not *complected*) man.

compliment, complement. *Compliment* means "to express praise": He *complimented* Beatrice on her good taste.

Complement means "to complete, enhance, or bring to perfection": The illustrations should *complement* the text. The nouns *compliment* and *complement* are distinguished similarly.

connect up. Redundant; omit *up*: We *connected* (not *connected up*) our new range.

considerable. Colloquial as a noun; correct as an adjective to indicate amount; incorrect when used for the adverb *considerably*:

COLLOQUIAL: He lost *considerable* in the stock market.

CORRECT: She had *considerable* influence.

CORRECT: They were *considerably* interested in his plan.

contact. *Contact* as a verb meaning "to get in touch with" is still not acceptable in formal writing. *Contact* as a noun meaning "source" has become accepted.

continual, continuous. *Continual* means "frequently repeated": He worked in spite of *continual* interruptions.

Continuous means "without interruption": We heard the *continuous* roar of the falls.

continued on. Often redundant; omit *on*: We *continued* (not *continued on*) our journey. But: We *continued on* Highway 280.

correspond to, correspond with. *Correspond to* means "to be similar or analogous": Our Parliament *corresponds to* the U.S. Congress.

Correspond with means "to be in agreement or conformity": Her actions did not *correspond with* her intentions.

Correspond with also means "to communicate through exchange of letters."

council, counsel, consul. *Council* means "a deliberative assembly of persons": The city *council* convenes at noon.

Counsel (noun) means "advice" or "attorney": He gave me good *counsel* when he told me to stop procrastinating. The *counsel* for the defense was a noted lawyer.

Counsel (verb) means "to give advice": He will *counsel* me about postgraduate plans.

Consul means "an officer in the foreign service": The distinguished guest was the *consul* from Spain.

credible, credulous, creditable. *Credible* means "believable": A good witness should be *credible*.

Credulous means "too ready to believe" or "gullible": A *credulous* person is easily duped.

Creditable means "praiseworthy": The young pianist gave a *creditable* performance of a difficult work.

data, phenomena, strata, media. These are plural forms: Those *data* are available. The singular forms are *datum* (rarely used), *phenomenon, stratum, medium*.

different from, different than. Formal usage requires *different from*: Her dress is *different from* yours. The tendency is growing, however, to accept *different than* when a clause follows, since it seems simpler: Is your address *different than* (rather than *different from what*) it was last year?

differ from, differ with. *Differ from* expresses unlikeness: This book *differs from* the others in giving more details.

Differ with expresses divergence of opinion: I *differ with* you about the importance of the tax bill.

discover, invent. *Discover* means "to find something already existing but not known": Balboa was the first European to *discover* the Pacific.

Invent means "to create or originate": Samuel F. B. Morse *invented* the telegraph.

disinterested, uninterested. *Uninterested* means simply "not interested": Pat is *uninterested* in mechanics.

Disinterested means "not influenced by personal interest; impartial, unbiased": Only a truly *disinterested* person should serve as an arbitrator.

dived, dove. *Dived* is the preferred past tense and past participle of *dive*: The youngsters *dived* (not *dove*) for coins.

due (to). *Due to* as a preposition is common in informal use but not in formal use; use *because of* instead: We were late *because of* (not *due to*) traffic.

Due is an adjective; it may correctly follow a linking verb: Our lateness was *due to* traffic.

each other, one another. *Each other* refers to *two* persons or things, *one another* to *three or more.*

effect. See *affect.*

emigrate, immigrate. *Emigrate* means "to leave a country"; *immigrate* means "to enter a new country": Millions *emigrated* from Europe. They *immigrated* to Canada.

end up. Often redundant. The game *ended* (not *ended up*) in a tie. Use it only where you must: He *ended up* a convict.

enthuse. Colloquial for *become enthusiastic:* She *becomes enthusiastic* (not *enthuses*) about everything.

everyone. See *anyone.*

everyplace, everywheres. See *anyplace, anywheres.*

every so often. Colloquial for *occasionally.* Also colloquial: *every which way, every bit as, every once in a while.*

except. See *accept.*

fact. See *actual fact.*

famous, notable, notorious. *Famous* means "widely known"; it usually has favorable connotations.

Notable means "worthy of note" or "prominent": A person can be *notable* without being *famous.*

Notorious means "widely known in an unfavorable way": Bluebeard was *notorious* for being a bad husband.

farther, further. *Farther* refers to distance: He walked *farther* than I did.

Further means "to a greater extent or degree": Let's discuss the matter *further.*

fewer, less. Use *fewer* with countable things; *fewer* refers to number: She has *fewer* assets than I have.

Use *less* with things that are not countable but are considered in bulk or mass; *less* refers to quantity: She has *less* money than I have.

fine. The adjective *fine* is much overused as a vague word of approval, as "a *fine* boy." Use a more precise word. As an adverb meaning "well" ("He does *fine*"), it is colloquial. *Fine* means "subtle; not coarse."

folks. Colloquial for *family, relatives, people.*

former, first; latter, last. *Former* and *latter* refer to the first and second named of two; *first* and *last* refer to items in a series.

funny. Do not use in formal writing to mean "odd" or "peculiar."

generally always. *Generally* means "ordinarily"; thus *generally always* is contradictory and incorrect: She *generally* (or *generally, if not always*—not *generally always*) swims before breakfast.

good. Do not use this adjective for the adverb *well:* The car runs *well* (not *good*).

As an adjective, *good* may correctly follow a linking verb: She feels *good* about winning. See G-5.1–5.3, page 5.

had of. Incorrect for *had:* I wish I *had* (or I'd—not I *had of* or I'*d of*) seen the show.

had ought. Incorrect for *ought:* I *ought* (not *had ought*) to go.

Hadn't ought is also incorrect. Use *ought not.*

hanged, hung. *Hanged* means "executed": Judas *hanged* himself.

Hung means "suspended": The picture was *hung.*

have got. Colloquial for *have:* I *have* (not *have got*) a dollar.

healthy, healthful. *Healthy* means "possessing health": The children are *healthy.*

Healthful means "conducive to health": Good food is *healthful.*

heighth. Incorrect for *height:* He was of medium *height* (not *heighth*).

herself, himself. See *myself.*

hopefully. Strictly, it means "full of hope": Christy *hopefully* awaited the posting of grades. In formal use, avoid it in the sense of "it is hoped that": *We hope that* (not *Hopefully*) the train will arrive on time.

imply, infer. The writer or speaker *implies*; the reader or listener *infers.*

Imply means "to state indirectly or suggest": He *implied* that we were at fault.

Infer means "to draw a conclusion or derive by reasoning": I *inferred* from his statement that he blamed us.

in, into. *Into* indicates movement from outside to inside: Fido ran *into* the house.

Otherwise, use *in*: Fido stays *in* the house at night.

in back of. Colloquial for *behind, at the back of, back of.*

individual, person, party. Do not use *party* or *individual* when you mean simply *person*: *A person* (not *an individual* or *a party*) that I met told me the news.

Except in legal and telephone-company language, and when you mean "one taking part," do not use *party* to refer to one person.

Use *individual* only when emphasizing a person's singleness: Will you act with the group or as an *individual*?

ingenious, ingenuous. *Ingenious* means "clever"; *ingenuous* means "naive, frank."

in regards to. Incorrect for *in regard to, with regards to,* or *as regards.*

inside of. Often redundant; omit *of* or use *within*: He was *inside* (not *inside of*) the room.

Inside of is colloquial when used in reference to time or distance: I shall come *within* (not *inside of*) an hour. I was *within* (not *inside of*) a mile of my destination.

"The *inside* of the house" is correct; here *inside* is a noun.

instance, instant, instant's. *Instance* means "a case or example": He cited an *instance* of discrimination.

Instant (noun) means "a brief time, a particular point in time, a moment": Come here this *instant!*

Instant (adjective) means "urgent or immediate": An *instant* need is food for the poor. Do you like *instant* coffee?

Instant's. Possessive form of the noun *instant*: He came at an *instant's* notice.

invent. See *discover.*

irregardless. An incorrect combination of *irrespective* and *regardless*:

WRONG: *Irregardless* of the cost, I shall go.

RIGHT: *Regardless* of the cost, I shall go.

RIGHT: *Irrespective* of the cost, I shall go.

is when, is where. Avoid both expressions except when referring to a time or place:

WRONG: A treaty *is when* nations sign an agreement.

RIGHT: A treaty *is* a signed agreement among nations.

RIGHT: Home *is where* the heart is. [place]

it being. An awkward substitute for *since it is.*

its, it's. *Its* is the possessive of *it:* The dog wagged *its* tail.

It's is the contraction of *it is.* Use *it's* only if you can correctly substitute *it is* in your sentence: *It's* (*it is*) the best thing.

kid, kids. Colloquial for *children* or *young people.*

kind of, sort of. Colloquial if used for *somewhat* or *rather.*

kind of a, sort of a. Omit the *a.* He wanted *some kind of* (not *some kind of a*) book.

last. See *former.* See also *later.*

later, latter. *Later,* the comparative form of *late,* means "more late."

Latter refers to the second of two things mentioned. If more than two are mentioned, use *last* instead of *latter.*

lead, led. *Lead* (rhymes with *need*) is the present tense of the verb meaning "to conduct, to go at the head of, to show the way": She will *lead* us to safety.

Led is the past tense and past participle of the same verb: She *led* us to safety. She has *led* us to safety.

Lead (rhymes with *dead*) is a metal: I need a *lead* pipe.

learn, teach. *Learn* means "to acquire knowledge": We *learned* irregular verbs.

Teach means "to impart knowledge": The professor *taught* us irregular verbs.

leave, let. *Leave* means "to depart": I must *leave* now. *Let* means "to permit": *Let* me go.

less. See *fewer*.

liable, likely. See *apt*.

lie, lay. *Lie* means "to rest" and is an intransitive verb (it never takes an object): He makes me *lie* down in green pastures. The islands *lie* under the tropical sun. Here *lies* Jeremiah Todd.

Lay means "to put" or "to place" and is a transitive verb (it must take an object): *Lay* your *head* on this pillow. Let me *lay* your *fears* to rest.

To complicate matters, the past tense of *lie* is spelled and pronounced the same as the present tense of *lay*:

Present	Past	Past Participle
lie [rest]	lay [rested]	(has) lain [rested]
lay [place]	laid [placed]	(has) laid [placed]

Yesterday Sandra *lay* [*rested*] too long in the sun. She should not have *lain* [*rested*] there so long. Yesterday the workers *laid* [*placed*] the foundation. They have *laid* [*placed*] it well.

like, as. In formal English, do not use *like* (preposition) where *as* or *as if* (conjunction) sounds right: He sounds *as if* (not *like*) he's angry. She died just *as* (not *like*) her mother did.

loose, lose. *Loose* (usually adjective—rhymes with *goose*) is the opposite of *tight* or *confined*: A *loose* coupling caused the wreck. Help! The lions are *loose*!

Loose is also sometimes a verb: *Loose* my bonds.

Lose (verb—rhymes with *use*) is the opposite of *to find* or *win*: Did you *lose* your wallet? We may *lose* the game.

lots, lots of. Colloquial if used for *much* or *many*.

mad, angry. In formal English, do not use *mad* to mean "angry." The common formal meaning of mad is "insane" or "insanely foolish": Do not be *angry* with me (not *mad* at me).

many, much. *Many* refers to numbers; *much* refers to quantities: *Many* students derive *much* pleasure from extracurricular activities.

marvelous. Overused as a vague word of approval.

may. See *can*.

maybe, may be. *Maybe* is an adverb meaning "perhaps": *Maybe* you should ask her. Do not confuse it with the verb *may be*: He *may be* arriving late tonight.

media. See *data*.

meet up with. Redundant; omit *up with*: I *met* (not *met up with*) my friends in the cafeteria.

moral, morale. *Moral* (as an adjective) means "righteous or ethical": To pay his debts was a *moral* obligation.

Moral (as a noun) means "a lesson or truth taught in a story": the *moral* of the story is that greed is wrong.

Morale is a noun meaning "spirit": The team's *morale* sagged.

most, almost. Do not use the adjective *most* for the adverb *almost*. *Almost* (not *most*) all my friends came.

myself, yourself, himself, herself. Do not substitute these intensive-reflexive pronouns for the personal pronouns *I, you, him, her*: Grace and *you* (not *yourself*) are invited. She sent tickets to Don and *me* (not *myself*).

See G-6.5, page 6.

nauseated, nauseous. *Nauseated* means "suffering from nausea": The fumes made me *nauseated*.

Nauseous means "causing nausea": The *nauseous* fumes overcame me.

nice. Trite and overused as a substitute for *pleasant* or *agreeable* or for indicating approval. Use a specific adjective.

no account, no good. Colloquial for *worthless* or *useless*.

notable, notorious. See *famous*.

nothing else but. Colloquial for *nothing but*.

noplace, nowheres. See *anyplace, anywheres*.

nowhere near. Colloquial for *not nearly*.

number. See *amount*.

of. *Of* is incorrect when used for *have* in such combinations as *should have, could have, may have, ought to have*.

off of. Usually redundant; omit *of*: Keep *off* (not *off of*) the grass. He jumped *off* (not *off of*) the platform.

See *all of* for another redundant use of *of*.

O.K. Colloquial for *all right* or *correct*.

one another. See *each other*.

only. Place *only* as close as possible to the word it modifies, to prevent misreading: He *has only* (not *only has*) one book.

oral. See *verbal*.

ought to of. Nonstandard for *ought to have*. See *of*.

out loud. Colloquial for *aloud*: Read the passage *aloud*.

outside of. Colloquial for *besides, except*. *Of* is redundant when denoting space: She was *outside* (not *outside of*) the store. But "the *outside of* the house" is correct; here *outside* is a noun.

over with. Redundant; omit *with*.

party, person. See *individual*.

phenomena. See *data*.

plan on. Do not use in formal English for *plan to*: I *plan to* go (not *plan on going*).

plenty. Colloquial when used as an adverb: His excuse was *quite* (not *plenty*) good enough for me.

Plenty is correct as a noun: We have *plenty* of food.

practical, practicable. *Practical* means "useful, sensible, not theoretical"; *practicable* means "feasible, capable of being put into practice": Because they were *practical* men, they submitted a plan that was *practicable*.

pretty. Colloquial for *large*: The accident will cost him a *large* (not *pretty*) sum.

principle, principal. A *principle* is a rule or a truth (remember: *principLE* = *ruLE*): The Ten Commandments are moral *principles*. The Pythagorean theorem is a mathematical *principle*.

Elsewhere, use *principal*, meaning "chief, chief part, chief person": All *principal* roads are closed. At 8 percent, your *principal* will earn $160 interest. The *principal* praised the students.

proven. *Proved* is the preferred past participle of *prove*. *Proven* may be used adjectivally: She is a *proven* actress.

provided, providing. Use *provided* (*that*) in preference to *providing* (*that*) when you mean "on the specific condition that": She will donate twenty dollars *provided that* (not *providing that*) her employer matches it.

put over, put across, put in. *Put over* and *put across* are colloquial when they mean "accomplish against opposition." *Put in* is colloquial for "spend":

COLLOQUIAL: He *put across* his ideas.

FORMAL: He succeeded in having his ideas accepted.

raise, rise. *Raise, raised, raised* is a transitive verb (takes an object): He *raises* vegetables. He *raised* the window.

Rise, rose, risen is an intransitive verb (never has an object): The sun is *rising*.

range, vary. *Range* means "to change or differ within limits": Applicants *ranged* in age from nineteen to thirty years.

Vary means "to change or differ": Applicants *varied* in age.

rarely ever. An incorrect joining of *rarely* and *hardly ever*.

real. Colloquial when used for the adverb *really* or *very*: He was *very* (not *real*) brave.

reason is because. Use a noun clause instead: The reason he is late is *that* (not *because*) he overslept. [Or *He is late because he overslept*.]

refer. See *allude, refer*.

regardless, regards. See *irregardless, in regards to*.

respectfully, respectively. *Respectfully* means "in a manner showing respect": He bowed *respectfully* before the queen. *Respectfully* yours.

Respectively means "each in the order given": First and second prizes were awarded to Luann and Juan, *respectively*.

Reverend. Never use *Reverend* alone as a form of address. The title *Reverend* is properly preceded by *the* and is followed by *Mr.* or by the first name or initials of the person referred to: We met the *Reverend* Charles Harris (or the *Reverend Mr. Harris*).

right. Colloquial or archaic when used to mean "directly" or "very": She went *directly* (not *right*) home. He was *very* (not *right*) tired.

round. See *about*.

see where. Incorrect if used for *see that*: I *see that* (not *see where*) the tax bill was passed.

seeing as how, seeing that. Incorrect for *since* or *because*.

seldom ever. Redundant and incorrect for *seldom, hardly ever, seldom if ever, seldom or never*.

shape. Colloquial if used for *condition*: He was in poor *condition* (not *shape*).

should of. Incorrect for *should have*. See *of*.

sight. See *cite*.

since. See *as, because, since*.

sit, set. *Sit, sat, sat* is an intransitive verb (has no object); it means "to be seated": I *sat* on the floor.

Set, set, set is a transitive verb (has an object) and means "to put or place": She *set* the dishes on the table.

(*Set* has several intransitive senses, but it is equivalent to *sit* only when one speaks of a hen that *sets* on her eggs.)

so. *So* is informal when used to introduce a main clause; use *therefore* or recast the sentence:

INFORMAL: The day was warm, *so* we rested.

FORMAL: The day was warm; *therefore* we rested.

GENERALLY ACCEPTABLE: *Because* the day was warm, we rested.

Avoid *so* for *very*: I am *very* (not *so*) happy.

Avoid using *so* for *so that* in clauses of purpose: She came *so that* (not *so*) she might help.

some. Colloquial if used for *somewhat, a little*, or *quite*: He worried *somewhat* (not *some*). He's *quite a* (not *some*) golfer!

somebody, someone. See *anyone*.

someplace, somewheres. See *anyplace, anywheres*.

sort of, sort of a. See *kind of, kind of a*.

strata. See *data*.

such, no such a. *Such* is colloquial when used for *very*: It is *such* a lovely day. BETTER: It is a *very* lovely day.

When *such* suggests "what kind" or "how much," it is followed in formal writing by a clause specifying the degree or kind: It was *such* a lovely day *that we went on a picnic*. We saw *such* clouds *that we came home*.

No such a is incorrect for *no such*. There is *no such* (not *no such a*) place.

sure. Do not use the adjective *sure* for the adverb *surely* or *certainly*: I *surely* (not *sure*) admire her.

COLLOQUIAL: "Are you going?" "*Sure*."

sure and. See *try and*.

suspicion. Do not use this noun for the verb *suspect*: I *suspect* (not *suspicion*) that he took your watch.

take. See *bring*.

take and, went and. Redundant: He *hit* (not *took and hit* or *went and hit*) the ball.

teach. See *learn*.

terribly. Colloquial when used for *extremely* or *very*: It's *very* (not *terribly*) late.

than, then. *Than* is a conjunction suggesting difference: He is taller *than* I (am tall). See also *different from*.

Then is an adverb meaning "next" or "in that case": *Then* we shall go.

that. See *this* and *who*.

that there. See *this here*.

their, there, they're. *Their* is a possessive pronoun: It is *their* turn.

There is an adverb referring to place: Sit *there*. It is also an expletive (an introductory word): *There* are four of us.

They're is a contraction of *they are*: *They're* on their way.

these kind, these sort. *Kind* and *sort* are singular nouns. Do not modify them with the plurals *these* and *those*. Use the singular *this* or *that* instead: I prefer *this* (not *these*) kind of fish. *That* sort (not *those* sort) of fish will make me sick.

thing. Avoid this vague noun when you can use a more specific one: Her next *point* (not *The next thing she said*) concerned economic benefits.

this, that, which. Use only to refer to a definite antecedent. See G-6.13, page 7.

this here, that there, these here, those there. Nonstandard for *this, that, these, those*.

those kind. See *these kind*.

thusly. Incorrect for *thus*.

to, too, two. *To* is a preposition: She came *to* class. *To* also introduces an infinitive: I wanted *to* hear him.

Too is an adverb meaning "also" or expressing degree: She laughed *too*. He was *too* sick to work. Do not use *too* for *very*: He did not look *very* (not *too*) happy.

Two is a number: I have *two* books.

try and, sure and. Incorrect for *try to* and *sure to*: Try *to* (not *Try and*) come. Be *sure to* (not *sure and*) call me.

unique. *Unique* means "having no like or equal." Do not use it with *more, most, very*, or the like: The design was *unique* (not *most unique*).

up. Often redundant. See *connect up, end up, meet up*.

usually always. Incorrect for *usually* or *usually, if not always*. See *generally always*.

vary. See *range*.

verbal, oral, aural. *Verbal* means "expressed in words, either written or spoken": An artist's expression may take pictorial, plastic, *verbal*, or other form. (For the grammatical term *verbal*, see G-4.6, page 4.)

Oral means "uttered or spoken": He gave an *oral* report.

Aural refers to hearing ("of or perceived by the ear"): Everyone has an *oral* (speaking), *aural* (hearing), and reading vocabulary.

very. Do not use this adverb to modify a past participle directly. Use *very* + an adverb such as *much, well*: Her singing was *very much* appreciated (not *very* appreciated).

Avoid overuse of *very*. *Extremely* and *quite* are good synonyms: She was *quite* (not *very*) embarrassed.

wait on. *Wait on* means "to attend or serve." It is colloquial if used to mean *wait for*: I waited *for* (not *on*) a bus.

want in, out, down, off, etc. Colloquial for *want to come in, want to go out*, etc.

way, ways. *Way* is colloquial if used for *away*: He lives *away* (not *way*) across the valley.

Way is colloquial in reference to health: He is in poor health (not *in a bad way*).

Ways is colloquial for *way* when indicating distance: He lives a little *way* (not *ways*) down the road.

weird. Slang when used for *strange, unusual*.

went and. See *take and*.

where. Incorrect when used for *that*. I read in the paper *that* (not *where*) she had arrived.

where . . . at. See *at*.

which. See *who* and *this*.

while. The strict meaning of *while* is "during the time that." Avoid using it to mean *and, but, though*, or *whereas*: A century ago many criminals were executed in America, *whereas* (not *while*) today very few are.

who, which, that. Use *who*, not *which*, when referring to people; *which* is only for things. *That* can refer to people or things: The people *who* (or *that*, but not *which*) live here are noisy.

Who may introduce either a restrictive or nonrestrictive clause (see P-1.5b, page 13, for definitions of these terms). *That* introduces only restrictive clauses. Some authorities say that *which* should introduce only nonrestrictive clauses, as in "Healy Hall, *which* is on your right, was built in 1878." Other authorities see no harm in using it restrictively: The hall *which* is on your right was built in 1878.

with. Often redundant; see *over with*.

wonderful. Trite and overused as an adjective of approval.

worst way. Incorrect for *very much*: I want *very much* to go (not *I want to go in the worst way*).

would of. Incorrect for *would have*.

you was. Nonstandard for *you were*.

yourself. See *myself*.

Documentation: Citations and Bibliography

The Modern Language Association's new rules state that documentary footnotes (those that cite sources of your information) are not needed in a research paper or in an article intended for publication. Instead, you, the writer, need only refer parenthetically in your text to each source of information. Let us say that you wish to quote or paraphrase a comment from David Bercuson's book *Canada and the Burden of Unity*. You cite, in your text, the author's last name followed by the number of the page from which you took the information:

Direct quotation: Bercuson notes that many Canadians ''wish regionalism would go away'' (1). OR Commenting sadly, Bercuson adds that ''many Canadians who should know better wish regionalism would go away.'' (1).

Paraphrase or summary: Bercuson notes that many persons accept Canada's regionalism only reluctantly (1). OR Canada's regionalism has been accepted only reluctantly (Bercuson, 1).

Your reader can find full information on the book by turning to your bibliography:

Bercuson, David Jay. <u>Canada and the Burden of Unity.</u> Toronto: Macmillan of Canada, 1977.

NOTE: If you have more than one book by Bercuson in your bibliography, use an abbreviated title before the page number: (Bercuson, <u>Unity</u> 1).

Use the following forms for entries in a bibliography or list of works cited. (Underline to indicate italics.)

TYPE	ENTRY
BOOKS	
One author	Richler, Mordecai. *The Apprenticeship of Duddy Kravitz*. Toronto: McClelland & Stewart, 1969.
Two authors	Dobbs, Kildare, and Marjorie Harris. *Historic Canada*. Toronto: Methuen, 1984.
Three authors	Vance, F. R., J. R. Jowsey, and J. S. McLean. *Wildflowers Across the Prairies*. Saskatoon: Western Producer Prairie Books, 1984.
More than three authors	Alexander, David G., et al. *Atlantic Canada and Confederation: Essays in Canadian Political Economy*. Toronto: University of Toronto Press, 1983.
Editor	Petrone, Penny, ed. *First People First Voices*. Toronto: University of Toronto Press, 1983.
Author and editor	Layton, Irving. *Selected Poems*. Ed. Wynne Francis. Toronto: McClelland & Stewart, 1969.
Edition	McInnis, Edgar. *Canada: A Political and Social History*. 4th ed. Toronto: Holt, Rinehart and Winston of Canada, 1982.
Several volumes	Lindsey, Charles. *The Life and Times of William Lyon Mackenzie*. 2 vols. Toronto: Coles Publishing, 1979.
Essay or article in a collection	Smith, David E. "Western Politics and National Unity." *Canada and the Burden of Unity*. Ed. David J. Bercuson. Toronto: Macmillan of Canada, 1977.
Bulletin or government publication	Communications Branch of Indian and Northern Affairs Canada. *Canada's North: The Reference Manual*. Ottawa: Canadian Government Publishing Centre, 1983.
ENCYCLOPEDIA ARTICLES	
Signed	Weir, T. R. "Manitoba." *The Canadian Encyclopedia*, 1985 ed.
Initialed (identified in key)	Lyons, John. "Linguistics." *Encyclopedia Britannica: Macropedia*, 1979 ed.
Unsigned	"Yamaska River." *Encyclopedia Canadiana*, 1972 ed.
PERIODICAL ARTICLES	
Magazine article (signed)	Silver, Jim. "The Erosion of Medicare." *Canadian Dimension*. May 1984:9–11.
Magazine article (unsigned)	"Converter Turns Text Into Speech Output." *Canadian Datasystems*. Sept. 1982:21.
Journal article (consecutive paging throughout volume)	Granetstein, J. L. "Culture and Scholarship: The First Ten Years of the Canada Council." *The Canadian Historical Review* 45.4(1984):441–474. [45.4 means vol. 45, number 4.]
Journal article (new paging each issue)	Whitaker, Reg. "Turner and the Trudeau Legacy." *Canadian Forum* 64 (1984):6–8.
Newspaper article (signed)	Valentine, Robert. "Merchant Fears the Worst from Museum Expansion." *Montreal Gazette* 18 Dec. 1985:B-3.
Newspaper article or editorial (unsigned)	"Too Many Are In Jail." Editorial. *Montreal Gazette* 18 Dec. 1985:B-2.
Review of book, etc.	Smith, Rowland. Rev. of *Book of Mercy*, by Leonard Cohen. *Canadian Literature* Spring 1985:155–6.
UNPUBLISHED AND MISCELLANEOUS	
Doctoral dissertation or Master's thesis	Guy, R. M. "The Industrial Development and Urbanization of Pictou County, Nova Scotia to 1900." M.A. Thesis, Acadia University, 1962.
Paper read but not published; lecture; interview	Waterman, A. M. C. "The Canadian Fallacy." Paper presented to the Seventh Annual Meeting of the Canadian Economic Association, Kingston, June 1983. Pechter, Edward. Personal interview. 6 April 1985.
Television or radio programme	*The Great Canadian Culture Hunt*. Producer/director Robert Patchell. CBC. CBMT, Montreal. 26 July 1976.
Computer software	Arctic Data Corp. *Arctic Data Accounting*. Computer software. Arctic Data Corp., 1985.